DOUBLED AND VENERABLE

Also by Terence Reese and David Bird

MIRACLES OF CARD PLAY

UNHOLY TRICKS
More Miraculous Card Play

Doubled and Venerable

Further Miracles of Card Play

TERENCE REESE and DAVID BIRD

LONDON
VICTOR GOLLANCZ LTD
in association with Peter Crawley
1987

First published in Great Britain 1987
by Victor Gollancz Ltd,
14 Henrietta Street, London WC2E 8QJ

© Terence Reese and David Bird 1987

British Library Cataloguing in Publication Data
Reese, Terence
 Doubled and venerable : further miracles
 of card play.
 1. Contract bridge—Anecdotes, facetiae,
 satire, etc.
 I. Title II. Bird, David, *1946–*
 795.41′5′0207   GV1282.32

 ISBN 0–575–03960–4

ACKNOWLEDGEMENT

The authors are, as usual, indebted to the editors of *Bridge International*, *International Popular Bridge Monthly* and *Bridge World* (USA) for permission to reprint stories that have appeared in their columns.

Photoset and printed in Great Britain by
WBC Print Ltd, Bristol

Contents

At the Monastery of St. Titus

The Abbot:	A capable but uninspired player; greatly jealous of his reputation.
Brother Lucius:	The monastery's chief accountant and its most cunning and deceptive card player.
Brother Xavier:	Monastery barber for the past twenty years; an admirer of Brother Lucius and a good player.
Brother Paulo:	An Italian monk transferred to St. Titus to strengthen the first team.
Brother Aelred:	The monastery organist; a weak but aspiring player.
Brother Damien:	A promising postulant, keen to make his mark on the monastery bridge scene.

In the African Jungle

Brother Tobias:	A missionary who has successfully converted the Bozwambi tribe to the Acol system.
Brother Luke:	Right-hand man of Brother Tobias, but his keenest rival at the table.
The Parrot:	Protégé of Brother Luke; has far outdistanced him in skill.
The Witchdoctor:	A wild overbidder, much feared by the other natives, who never dare double him.
Mbozi:	Docile and lazy during the play but extremely fierce in the post-mortem.
Mrs. Okoku:	Captain of the Bozwambi Ladies team and a sturdy player.
Miss Nabooba:	A slender 20-year-old who has fulfilled her early promise.

PART I

At the Monastery of St. Titus

1

The Instruction of Brother James

Every Wednesday evening, in the hour preceding supper, the Abbot held a cardplay class for members of the novitiate. Although attendance was not actually compulsory, no novice had ever put this matter to the test.

"Now, here's an interesting four-spade contract," said the Abbot, chalking a diagram on the blackboard.

A bell sounded in the distance, summoning the monks to the supper table.

"West leads the king of diamonds," continued the Abbot, "and you. . ."

"Excuse me, Abbot," said Brother Mark in the front row. "Isn't that the supper bell?"

"Six o'clock already?" grunted the Abbot. "Very well. Everyone take down the deal before you go. I shall expect a full written analysis from each of you by next week."

As the Abbot was walking towards the refectory, Brother James approached him. "May I have a word with you, Abbot?" he said. "I feel I'm ready to try a session or two in the senior duplicate. I was wondering if you could recommend one of the senior monks who might be willing to partner me."

The Abbot turned and smiled warmly at Brother James, one of his most diligent pupils. "If you really want to learn about this game of ours," he said, "you can do no better than watch it played at the very highest level."

"I'm sure you're right, Abbot," replied Brother James.

"Yes, that's the way to do it," said the Abbot. "You must come and sit behind me in tonight's duplicate game."

Later that evening, in the senior cardroom, Brother James took a seat at the Abbot's elbow. This was the first deal:

Love all
Dealer South

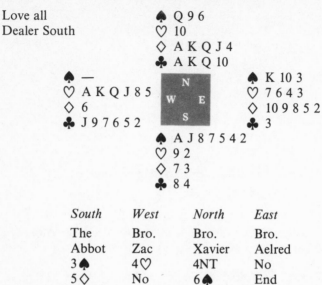

```
                    ♠ Q 9 6
                    ♡ 10
                    ◇ A K Q J 4
                    ♣ A K Q 10
♠ —                      N          ♠ K 10 3
♡ A K Q J 8 5       W         E     ♡ 7 6 4 3
◇ 6                      S          ◇ 10 9 8 5 2
♣ J 9 7 6 5 2                       ♣ 3
                    ♠ A J 8 7 5 4 2
                    ♡ 9 2
                    ◇ 7 3
                    ♣ 8 4
```

South	West	North	East
The	Bro.	Bro.	Bro.
Abbot	Zac	Xavier	Aelred
3♠	4♡	4NT	No
5◇	No	6♠	End

Brother Xavier had a difficult call over four hearts. Fearing that five spades would be taken as a request for a heart control, he resorted to Blackwood. When the Abbot admitted to an ace, Brother Xavier bid the slam.

The black-bearded Brother Zac led the ace of hearts and continued with the king, ruffed with dummy's ♠ 6. The Abbot, anxious not to start the evening with a bad board, turned his attention to the trump suit. His plan was to lead the queen of spades from dummy. If Brother Aelred, one of the weakest players in the monastery, did not cover with the king, he would try to drop the singleton king offside.

His mind made up, the Abbot called for the queen of trumps. It was covered by the king and ace, West discarding a heart.

Making a poor job of concealing his delight at this turn of events, the Abbot turned towards Brother James. "A little lucky, perhaps," he said. "But good players create their own luck. I would also have made it if West had held a singleton king, so it was an excellent slam."

Resuming his play of the hand, the Abbot returned to dummy with a club. His lead of ♠ 9 was not covered, so now he faced the problem of how to return to hand to draw the last trump. When he tried the king of clubs, Brother Aelred ruffed.

"I led a club," barked the Abbot, looking scornfully to his right. "Surely you must have some clubs left."

"I don't think so," said Brother Aelred, sorting painstakingly through his hand. "No, as far as I remember I only started with one."

"What a ludicrous distribution of the cards," exclaimed the Abbot. "Makes the game more like spinning a roulette wheel than a test of skill."

Brother James sat back in his chair, deep in thought. Why hadn't the Abbot unblocked the spade suit by ruffing with the *nine* at trick 2? It would certainly be very instructive to know why. Still, thought Brother James, I'd better ask him afterwards. I don't want to make a fool of myself.

The second deal was passed out. This was the last board of the round:

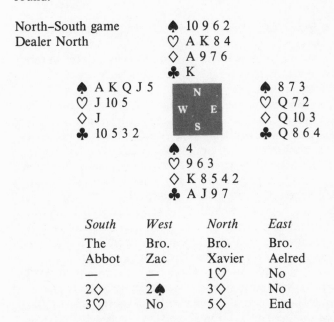

North–South game
Dealer North

	♠ 10 9 6 2	
	♡ A K 8 4	
	◇ A 9 7 6	
	♣ K	
♠ A K Q J 5		♠ 8 7 3
♡ J 10 5		♡ Q 7 2
◇ J		◇ Q 10 3
♣ 10 5 3 2		♣ Q 8 6 4
	♠ 4	
	♡ 9 6 3	
	◇ K 8 5 4 2	
	♣ A J 9 7	

South	West	North	East
The	Bro.	Bro.	Bro.
Abbot	Zac	Xavier	Aelred
—	—	1♡	No
2◇	2♠	3◇	No
3♡	No	5◇	End

Brother Zac started with the top two spades against five diamonds, the Abbot ruffing the second round. When two rounds of trumps revealed a trump loser, the Abbot played a club to the king and ruffed another spade. After discarding a heart on the ace of clubs, he ruffed a club and cashed the top hearts, leaving this end position:

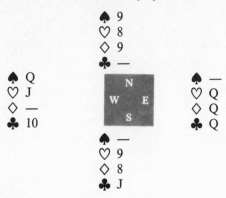

When ♠ 9 was led from dummy, East had no good answer. If he discarded the heart queen, declarer would ruff the spade and then ruff a club. Nor would it help to ruff dummy's spade with the queen of diamonds. Declarer would simply discard a heart and make his last two trumps separately.

Eventually Brother Aelred decided to discard the queen of clubs. The Abbot ruffed the spade, then led the established jack of clubs from hand. East had to ruff, so dummy's ◊ 9 won the last trick.

The Abbot turned triumphantly towards Brother James. "You see?" he said. "Didn't I tell you you'd see a thing or two at this table?"

"It was a beautiful end position, Abbot," replied Brother James. "I don't think I'll ever be able to play like that."

"Possibly not," agreed the Abbot, "but it is the duty of every one of us, the gifted and the ungifted, to develop his talents to the full."

"Move for the next round!" called a voice from across the room. "East–West pairs up one; boards down one."

"Ah!" exclaimed the Abbot. "These boards are going to Brother Lucius's table. You must go and watch when they get to the third deal, Brother James. See if Lucius gets the play right."

This was the bidding when the board was replayed:

South	West	North	East
Bro.	Bro.	Bro.	Bro.
Lucius	Damien	Paulo	Mark
—	—	1♡	No
2♡	2♠	No	No
3◊	No	5◊	End

Once more the two top spades were led against five diamonds. Brother Lucius ruffed the second round, drew one round of trumps with the ace and cashed the club king. He then crossed to the king of diamonds, finding that there was a trump loser.

Thanks to his foresight in unblocking the club king, he was a tempo ahead of the Abbot at this stage. After cashing the ace of clubs, he took three black-suit ruffs and cashed the top hearts. This was the end position:

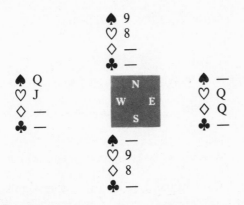

The ♠9 was led from dummy, promoting declarer's last trump. Twelve tricks were there.

Brother James considered the two lines of play he had seen. Lucius had played it better than the Abbot, hadn't he? Surely the Abbot's line had required East to hold the queen of clubs. Crossing back to the Abbot's table, he resumed his seat.

"Same contract, was it?" enquired the Abbot amiably.

Brother James nodded.

"And did he find my line of play?"

Brother James shook his head.

The Abbot smiled to himself. "And yet there are those who think that Brother Lucius is the best cardplayer in the monastery," he said. "Run over and tell Lucius I managed to make that diamond game, will you? If he wants to know how, I'll keep a spare seat for him at next Wednesday's class."

2

Brother Damien's Oriental Trick

Brother Lucius leaned towards the glowing fire and lifted some chestnuts off the grate with a pair of copper tongs. "Any more nuts for you, Abbot?" he said.

"Yes, I'll have a few more," replied the Abbot. "Not so large as last year's crop, are they?"

"No, they're hardly worth eating at this size," agreed Brother Lucius. "Did Xavier speak to you about this proposed match against the novitiate?"

"He did," replied the Abbot, juggling with a chestnut that was still too hot to handle. "Didn't think much of the idea myself. We'd be on a hiding to nothing, wouldn't we?"

"Well, it's most unlikely that they'd actually beat us," said Brother Lucius, somewhat amused at the Abbot's concern. "Still, one never can tell, after all the expert tuition you've given them."

The match was soon arranged. To give his side the maximum chance of overcoming any lucky breaks that might come the novices' way, the Abbot had insisted that a full 48 boards be played over two consecutive nights.

After evensong the following Tuesday a large crowd of kibitzers gathered in the novitiate cardroom. This hand occurred early in the first set of 12 boards.

East–West game
Dealer South

♠ A 9 6 4 3
♡ K 8 7 2
◇ J 5
♣ A K

♠ K Q J 2
♡ 10 9 5 3
◇ 10
♣ J 8 6 4

	N	
W		E
	S	

♠ 10 8 7
♡ 6
◇ Q 8 7 2
♣ Q 10 7 5 3

♠ 5
♡ A Q J 4
◇ A K 9 6 4 3
♣ 9 2

South	West	North	East
Bro.	The	Bro.	Bro.
Adam	Abbot	Cameron	Xavier
1◇	No	1♠	No
2♡	No	3♣	No
3◇	No	4NT	No
5♡	No	6♡	End

A nondescript auction from the novitiate pair never came close to investigating a grand slam. Against six hearts the Abbot led the king of spades, won by dummy's ace. Brother Adam cashed the ace and queen of trumps, East discarding a club on the second round.

Brother Adam nodded approvingly at the bad trump break. Good! That reduced the chance that Lucius and Paulo would make a grand in the other room. Now, how could he make sure of twelve tricks? He cashed the ace of diamonds and the 10 fell from West. Since it would obviously be disastrous if the king of diamonds were ruffed, he continued with a low diamond towards dummy's jack. West discarded a club but Brother Adam was unconcerned. Whatever East returned, he would be in control. If a spade came back he would ruff and lead good diamonds through West. If, instead, East returned a club he would win in the dummy, cross to the jack of trumps, and again play winning diamonds through West. He gave his partner a reassuring smile. The contract was cold.

"It's you to play," said Brother Xavier. "The lead's in the dummy."

"What?" exclaimed Brother Adam.

"The jack of diamonds won the trick," grunted the Abbot. "Come on."

It was no longer possible to make the contract. Declarer went through the motions of playing the remaining tricks but he eventually lost a spade and a heart, going one down.

Brother Adam turned admiringly towards Brother Xavier. "That was some defence, ducking the diamond," he said.

"Not too difficult," replied Brother Xavier. "You obviously didn't have a loser in spades or hearts or you would have played the diamonds from the top, hoping for a favourable break."

"Quite so, " said the Abbot, motioning impatiently for the next board to be brought into position. "Holding off the queen was obvious as the play had gone."

In the other room the monastery pair also came to a halt in six hearts:

South	West	North	East
Bro.	Bro.	Bro.	Bro.
Lucius	Damien	Paulo	Mark
1 ◇	No	1 ♠	No
2 ♡	No	4 ♣	No
4 ◇	No	4 ♠ .	No
5 ◇	No	6 ♣	No
6 ♡	End		

Brother Lucius was tempted to bid seven hearts at his final turn. The controls were certainly there but there might be some problem in establishing the diamond suit. Better to avoid borderline grands in a match like this, he thought.

Once more the king of spades lead was captured by the ace and declarer played the ace and queen of trumps, exposing the bad break. Brother Lucius now cashed the ace of diamonds, pausing for thought when the 10 appeared from West. "Jack, please," he said eventually.

His next move was to cross to the ace of clubs and lead ◇ 5, finessing the 9. Brother Damien ruffed and forced declarer with another spade but the contract was now secure. Brother Lucius ruffed a diamond with the king, setting up the suit, then crossed back to the jack of trumps, claiming the remainder.

If the finesse of ◇ 9 had lost to the queen, the contract would have been equally impregnable. Declarer would have ruffed the spade return and played winning diamonds through the West hand.

After 12 boards the novitiate team found themselves 22 IMPs adrift. They had the chance to reduce the margin on this deal early in the second set.

Game all
Dealer North

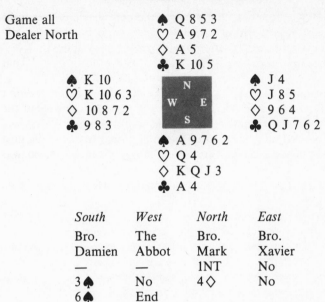

♠ Q 8 5 3
♡ A 9 7 2
◇ A 5
♣ K 10 5

♠ K 10
♡ K 10 6 3
◇ 10 8 7 2
♣ 9 8 3

♠ J 4
♡ J 8 5
◇ 9 6 4
♣ Q J 7 6 2

♠ A 9 7 6 2
♡ Q 4
◇ K Q J 3
♣ A 4

South	West	North	East
Bro.	The	Bro.	Bro.
Damien	Abbot	Mark	Xavier
—	—	1NT	No
3♠	No	4◇	No
6♠	End		

The novitiate pair plunged into a thin spade slam and the Abbot led ♣ 9. Brother Damien paused to assess his prospects. Even if there was only one trump loser, it was by no means obvious how he could avoid losing a heart trick.

How about an endplay? Yes, if the defender with the king of hearts also held K x or J 10 x in trumps it might be possible to endplay him. Brother Damien cashed the ace of trumps and the king of clubs. He then played three rounds of diamonds, discarding dummy's last club. These cards remained:

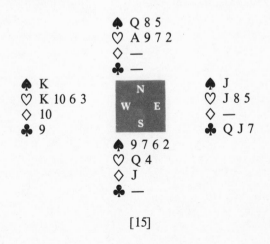

♠ Q 8 5
♡ A 9 7 2
◇ —
♣ —

♠ K
♡ K 10 6 3
◇ 10
♣ 9

♠ J
♡ J 8 5
◇ —
♣ Q J 7

♠ 9 7 6 2
♡ Q 4
◇ J
♣ —

[15]

Brother Damien now had to decide whether to lead a fourth round of diamonds before exiting in trumps.

"Come on, come on," muttered the Abbot. "Look at the time. It's past 10 already."

"I'm sorry, Abbot," said Brother Damien. "This is rather an interesting hand, though."

It seemed to Brother Damien that it would never cost to play the fourth round of diamonds. He led the jack of diamonds and the Abbot followed suit, presenting the young declarer with another problem. If West had the two major suit kings the winning play would be to ruff the diamond with dummy's queen. If East had the two kings, ruffing high would be a disastrous move. He would then lose two trump tricks.

Brother Damien could spot no clue to guide him on this crucial play. He therefore decided to play the Abbot for the two missing kings. Endplaying the Abbot would rank as a greater achievement among his colleagues. It would also make a more enjoyable spectacle for those watching. Brother Damien ruffed the jack of diamonds with the queen and exited with a trump to the Abbot's king. The Abbot's heart return was successfully run to the queen and the vulnerable slam was home.

Not a word was said as the two novices turned modestly to their scorecards. A few excited whispers came from the bystanders, who were obviously expecting a swing on the board.

"Would you be quiet!" said the Abbot, turning round crossly. "A simple endplay may be headline news in the novitiate. That's no justification for behaving like a cageful of parrots." He turned towards Brother Damien. "Just the twelve, was it?" he said.

A hand or two later Mark and Damien decided to press their luck with another delicate slam:

East–West game
Dealer South

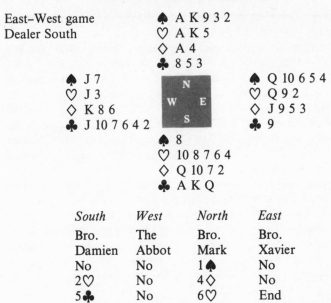

```
                    ♠ A K 9 3 2
                    ♡ A K 5
                    ◇ A 4
                    ♣ 8 5 3
♠ J 7                              ♠ Q 10 6 5 4
♡ J 3                              ♡ Q 9 2
◇ K 8 6                            ◇ J 9 5 3
♣ J 10 7 6 4 2                     ♣ 9
                    ♠ 8
                    ♡ 10 8 7 6 4
                    ◇ Q 10 7 2
                    ♣ A K Q
```

South	West	North	East
Bro.	The	Bro.	Bro.
Damien	Abbot	Mark	Xavier
No	No	1♠	No
2♡	No	4◇	No
5♣	No	6♡	End

The Abbot led the jack of clubs and Brother Damien won with the ace, noting the 9 from East. His heart sank as he surveyed the dummy. Perhaps he should have bid just four hearts with such poor trumps.

A second glance revealed that the hand was similar in a way to the slam he had made just a few moments before. If the defender with the third trump also held the diamond king, surely there might be a chance of endplaying him? No, that would require a miraculous lie of the cards and East's ♣ 9 at trick one had an ominous ring to it.

Another idea occurred to him. At trick 2 he made the bold play of the queen of diamonds from hand. The Abbot, placing declarer with Q J 10 or Q J 9 in the suit, played low and the queen held the trick. Holding his breath, Brother Damien cashed the ace and king of trumps. Both defenders followed.

"I must make twelve now," he said, in as casual a tone as he could muster. "I can discard one diamond loser and ruff the other. One of you makes a trump trick."

"Yes, another lucky one," declared the Abbot. "You needed a 3–2 trump break AND the king of diamonds onside. Well under fifty percent."

"You can say that again, Abbot," said Brother Xavier with a rueful smile. "He didn't have the jack of diamonds. I had it."

"Yes, I've you to thank for that one, Abbot," said Brother Damien. "You explained the Chinese finesse to us a couple of weeks ago, remember? You said it had a better chance of succeeding against a strong opponent because a weak opponent would cover the queen without thinking."

The Abbot eyed Brother Damien uncertainly. Was he being deliberately impertinent? Probably, but you could never tell. "Wake me up if it ever occurs to you to put the next board on the table, Brother Mark," he said.

Not surprisingly, Lucius and Paulo had bid neither of the two slams landed by Brother Damien. As a result, the novitiate team retired to their cells with an overall lead of 9 IMPs.

The following evening the senior cardroom was packed as the players took their seats. Even the most elderly kibitzers were hoping that the youngsters might somehow hold on to their lead.

There was not long to wait before the first slam hand:

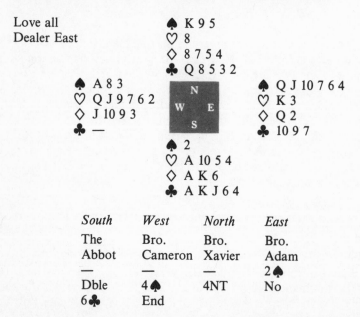

Love all
Dealer East

	♠ K 9 5	
	♡ 8	
	◇ 8 7 5 4	
	♣ Q 8 5 3 2	

♠ A 8 3
♡ Q J 9 7 6 2
◇ J 10 9 3
♣ —

♠ Q J 10 7 6 4
♡ K 3
◇ Q 2
♣ 10 9 7

♠ 2
♡ A 10 5 4
◇ A K 6
♣ A K J 6 4

South	West	North	East
The	Bro.	Bro.	Bro.
Abbot	Cameron	Xavier	Adam
—	—	—	2♠
Dble	4♠	4NT	No
6♣	End		

The Abbot could hardly do less at his second turn. His call of six clubs was passed out and West led the jack of diamonds.

"I'm afraid I was just looking for a sacrifice," said Brother Xavier, reluctant to display the dummy. "I've hardly anything for you."

"Yes, yes," grunted the Abbot. "Come on. Let's have a look at it."

Dummy, in fact, was quite suitable. If the ace of spades was onside, there was every chance of discarding a diamond on the king of spades and ruffing three hearts.

The Abbot won the first trick and cashed the ace of trumps. When West showed out, prospects were distinctly less rosy. East was marked with six spades and three clubs. Also, he must have at least two diamonds because West's opening lead had denied the queen. So East had at most two hearts and would be able to overruff the dummy if the Abbot played for three heart ruffs.

Fearing that he was in for a bad board, the Abbot played a second round of trumps, then led a spade towards dummy. West went in with the ace and exited with a low diamond, won by declarer. After the ace of hearts and a heart ruff, the Abbot cashed the king of spades and discarded a diamond. He then ruffed dummy's last spade. These cards were still at large:

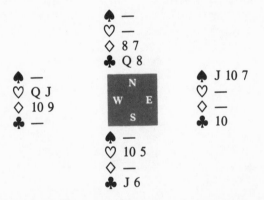

A heart lead now would obviously lead to defeat, so the Abbot tried the effect of the jack of clubs. Brother Cameron, sitting West, didn't like the look of this. Eventually he discarded the jack of hearts.

The Abbot blinked. There was only one more heart out, surely? He played ♣8 from dummy, then ruffed a heart with the queen. A diamond ruff to hand allowed him to cash the established heart. Twelve tricks were there.

"It was obvious I held four hearts, wasn't it?" said the Abbot, turning towards Brother Cameron with a puzzled expression. "You must have known that. Your partner's king came down on the second round."

"Yes, but what could I do?" replied Brother Cameron, his ill-assorted teeth protruding even more than usual. "If I throw a diamond, you can overtake your jack of trumps with the queen and ruff dummy's last diamond good."

Light dawned on the Abbot. "Do you think I didn't realise that?" he exclaimed. "Good gracious, I had the end position in mind virtually the moment the dummy went down."

"Not many people would have found my 4NT bid," observed Brother Xavier proudly.

"No," agreed the Abbot. "It was a poor call. Just as well I was on hand to rescue the situation."

With one twelve-board set still to be played, the senior team found they had moved into a 16 IMP lead.

"Hardly what one would call a respectable margin," declared the Abbot, with a stern glance at each of his team-mates. "There's still time to clock up something around the 50 IMP mark. We must spare no quarter in the final set."

The Abbot's instructions were fresh in Brother Paulo's mind when this hand was dealt.

Game all
Dealer South

```
                 ♠ J 4 2
                 ♡ A J 6 3
                 ◇ 7 6
                 ♣ J 7 6 2
   ♠ K 7 6                      ♠ A Q 8 3
   ♡ K 10 9 7 5      N          ♡ 8 2
   ◇ 8 5 2       W       E      ◇ J 10 9 3
   ♣ 9 4             S          ♣ Q 10 5
                 ♠ 10 9 5
                 ♡ Q 4
                 ◇ A K Q 4
                 ♣ A K 8 3
```

South	West	North	East
Bro.	Bro.	Bro.	Bro.
Paulo	Cameron	Lucius	Adam
1NT	No	2♣	No
2◇	No	2NT	No
3NT	End		

Against 3NT Brother Cameron led the ♡ 10 to the 3, 2 and queen. Since East had played the 2 fairly quickly, without giving the matter much consideration, Brother Paulo mentally placed the king of hearts with West. He next turned his attention to the club suit, obviously the key to the hand. If he cashed the ace-king and the queen fell, all would be well. If the queen was twice guarded, though, the other defender would have a chance to signal for spades when the third round of clubs was played.

At trick two Brother Paulo made the daring play of a low club from hand. Dummy's jack lost to the queen and East returned the jack of diamonds. Displaying no emotion, Brother Paulo won with the ace and finessed the jack of hearts successfully. When clubs proved to be 3–2 he had nine tricks.

"Oh, no! Did you have the king of spades?" asked Brother Adam, with an agitated glance at his partner.

Brother Cameron nodded.

"We have five tricks to take if I switch to a spade," continued Brother Adam. "I don't see how I can read that one; I couldn't believe he would play that way if the spades were bare." He turned towards Brother Paulo. "Why didn't you play clubs from the top? The queen might have dropped."

"Low club seemed very good chance," replied the Italian. "Nice possibility of slipping past queen-to-three with West, or even queen doubleton."

"Quite so," agreed Brother Lucius. "And if you do lose to the queen, it may be difficult for the defenders to find the right switch."

At the other end of the cardroom the Abbot and Brother Xavier had been dealt yet another slam hand.

North–South game

Dealer South

	♠ K 7 3	
	♡ A Q J 6 5 2	
	◇ A 10	
	♣ K 3	
♠ J 10 6 2		♠ —
♡ K 9	N	♡ 10 8 4
◇ 8 6 5	W E	◇ Q J 7 4 2
♣ J 9 6 4	S	♣ Q 10 8 7 5
	♠ A Q 9 8 5 4	
	♡ 7 3	
	◇ K 9 3	
	♣ A 2	

South	West	North	East
The	Bro.	Bro.	Bro.
Abbot	Damien	Xavier	Mark
1♠	No	3♡	No
3♠	No	4◇	No
5♣	No	5♡	No
6◇	No	6♠	End

The monastery team followed the modern style of not forcing on two-suiters. Brother Xavier's call of four diamonds was therefore a cue bid, probably agreeing spades as trumps. When Brother Xavier could not call six hearts over six diamonds, the Abbot deduced that the king of hearts was missing. Unwilling to bid a grand on a finesse, he settled for six spades.

Brother Damien, on lead, inspected his cards learnedly. It seemed to him that his hand fell into a category sometimes mentioned in erudite text-books. Since he had a trump trick that would probably come as a surprise to declarer, he should choose an opening lead that might put declarer to a premature decision. He extracted the 9 of hearts and down went the dummy.

The Abbot inspected the table's cards in a self-satisfied manner. Yes, the slam was an excellent one. Not that he had any intention of running into a heart ruff, of course. Perish the thought. "Ace of hearts," he instructed.

The Abbot now turned his attention to the trump suit. If West had all four trumps, nothing could be done. If East had four trumps, they could be picked up. "Play the *king* of spades, will you," he said, glancing at the kibitzers to check that his meticulous cardplay was receiving their full attention.

[22]

When East discarded on the first round of trumps the Abbot displayed a masterly lack of concern. "Queen of hearts," he said, trying to look like a man who had started with a singleton heart.

Brother Mark, sitting East, followed with a low heart, but the Abbot's momentary elation was soon quelled by the appearance of the king of hearts on his left. The slam was one down.

"Don't tell me," said Brother Xavier, with a pained shake of the head. "You gave them a talk on opening leads last week."

The last few boards passed without incident and the senior players were soon busy comparing scores.

"Minus 100," said the Abbot, hoping that by some miracle the slam hand might be flat.

"Oh dear," said Brother Lucius. "You played it in spades?"

The Abbot nodded.

"Well, they were in no-trumps, I'm afraid," continued Brother Lucius. "Minus 2220."

"What?" gasped the Abbot. "They were in the grand?"

"Yes," replied Brother Lucius. "Three spade tricks, six heart tricks and a couple of ace-kings. Thirteen on top when the hearts behave."

Across the room a frenzied addition was in progress.

"I don't think it's enough, is it?" said Brother Mark anxiously, "4, 5, 20 for the slam, that's 25, 26, 33 to us."

"Yes, and 1, 2, 14, 16, 21 to them," said Brother Damien, throwing his scorecard into the middle of the table. "I don't believe it! Fancy losing by just 4 IMPs after all those boards." A re-check of the totals gave the same depressing scoreline.

"The Abbot's team don't seem too pleased with the result either," observed Brother Adam. "Look at them."

Across the room a funereal silence reigned. Brother Paulo was polishing his spectacles and the Abbot was gazing bleakly at his scorecard.

The four novices smiled at each other, suddenly realising that losing by 4 IMPs was quite a triumph for them. There was always that 20 IMP slam swing to remember, too. The Abbot wouldn't forget that in a hurry.

"Come on, team," said Brother Damien. "Time for us to congratulate the winning captain."

3

Brother Paulo's Biltcliffe Coup

It was late August and the bridge season was about to start in earnest.
The Abbot had therefore arranged a few practice sessions for the
monastery first team. As always, these were being held in the Abbot's
study, where the chairs were more comfortable than those in the main
card-room. This was an early deal:

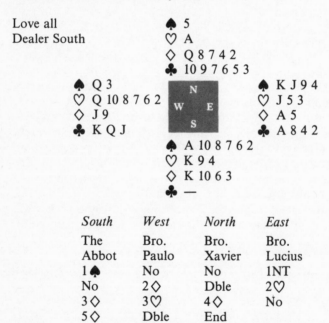

Love all
Dealer South

	♠ 5	
	♡ A	
	◇ Q 8 7 4 2	
	♣ 10 9 7 6 5 3	

♠ Q 3		♠ K J 9 4
♡ Q 10 8 7 6 2		♡ J 5 3
◇ J 9		◇ A 5
♣ K Q J		♣ A 8 4 2

	♠ A 10 8 7 6 2	
	♡ K 9 4	
	◇ K 10 6 3	
	♣ —	

South	West	North	East
The	Bro.	Bro.	Bro.
Abbot	Paulo	Xavier	Lucius
1♠	No	No	1NT
No	2◇	Dble	2♡
3◇	3♡	4◇	No
5◇	Dble	End	

Brother Paulo's two-diamond call was a transfer to hearts. Brother
Xavier, who was willing to compete to the three level in the minors,
doubled to show his diamonds. His intention was to bid three clubs
on the next round, should this be possible. The Abbot had a big fit for
diamonds and soon arrived in five diamonds doubled.

Brother Paulo looked no further than the king of clubs for his opening lead and the Abbot ruffed in hand. His plan now was to make as many trump tricks as possible. He crossed to the ace of hearts for a second club ruff, then cashed the ace of spades and ruffed a spade. After a third club ruff he cashed the king of hearts and ruffed a heart. The lead was in dummy and these cards remained:

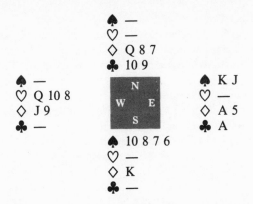

The Abbot ruffed a club with the king, then led a spade towards dummy. If West discarded on this trick, the Abbot intended to ruff with the 7 and exit with dummy's master club. Whichever defender ruffed, dummy's ◇ Q 8 would assure the Abbot of an eleventh trick.

In fact, Brother Paulo decided to ruff the spade with the 9. It was now the Abbot's turn to think. If he overruffed with the queen, that would be his last trick. A club exit would be ruffed low and the defenders would then score their high trumps separately. The Abbot therefore allowed West's 9 of trumps to win, discarding dummy's master club. When West now played a heart through, the Abbot ruffed with the 7 and East discarded a spade. Dummy's last two cards were the queen and 8 of diamonds, and the Abbot had to decide which card to play. Since East would doubtless have gone to four hearts holding:

      ♠ K J 9 4   ♡ Q J 5 3   ◇ A   ♣ A 8 4 2,

the Abbot eventually opted for the queen of diamonds. This pinned West's jack, establishing dummy's ◇ 8 as the eleventh trick.

"A dazzling effort, Abbot!" exclaimed Brother Xavier. "I thought I might have done a bit too much in the bidding."

The Abbot gave a short laugh. "I didn't hold back very much myself," he said. "That's the first Biltcliffe Coup for quite a while."

"Biltcliffe Coup?" queried Brother Paulo.

"Yes, haven't you heard of the term?" replied the Abbot. "A Biltcliffe Coup has four elements to it. First, the opponents must be about to play in a part score, but you keep the bidding open in the pass-out position. Secondly, the opponents must then bid to game. Thirdly you must double them, and fourthly they make the contract. If all that happens, it's called a Biltcliffe Coup."

"I see," said Brother Paulo, not sounding very impressed. "But why is it being called a Biltcliffe Coup?"

"Ah, well, you would never have met Brother Biltcliffe," continued the Abbot. "He once achieved the feat no less than three times in a single Gold Cup match. Ever since then, the coup has been called after him."

"Yes, I thought the term had passed into common usage," observed Brother Lucius. "I must check in the Bridge Player's Encyclopedia when I get back to my cell."

The rubber had advanced to game all when Brother Paulo was presented with a chance to gain his revenge.

Game all
Dealer West

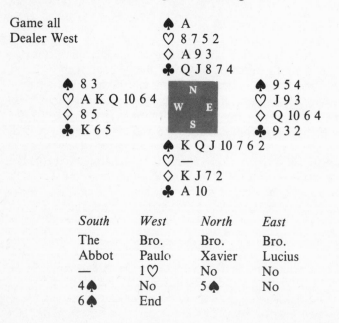

	♠ A	
	♡ 8 7 5 2	
	◇ A 9 3	
	♣ Q J 8 7 4	

♠ 8 3		♠ 9 5 4
♡ A K Q 10 6 4		♡ J 9 3
◇ 8 5		◇ Q 10 6 4
♣ K 6 5		♣ 9 3 2

	♠ K Q J 10 7 6 2	
	♡ —	
	◇ K J 7 2	
	♣ A 10	

South	West	North	East
The	Bro.	Bro.	Bro.
Abbot	Paulo	Xavier	Lucius
—	1♡	No	No
4♠	No	5♠	No
6♠	End		

Brother Paulo led the ace of hearts against six spades. The Abbot ruffed in hand, crossed to the ace of trumps, ruffed another heart and played three more rounds of trumps. Next came the ace and 10 of clubs.

Brother Paulo, sitting West, could see that the situation would be hopeless if he took this trick. He therefore allowed ♣ 10 to hold. The Abbot now had to play the diamond suit for one loser. His first move was to finesse dummy's ♦ 9, losing to East's 10. These cards remained:

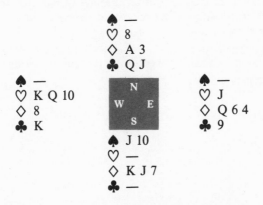

The Abbot ruffed the ♡ J return, Brother Paulo contributing the queen from the West seat. When the Abbot cashed the last trump, Brother Paulo continued his deception by discarding the king of hearts. East threw ♣ 9.

The Abbot crossed to the ace of diamonds and led another diamond towards his king–jack. East followed with a low card and the Abbot paused to check the evidence. It seemed from the fall of the cards that East's last card must be ♡ 10; West must hold the king of clubs and the queen of diamonds. With a confident flourish the Abbot tossed the king of diamonds on the table. Brother Paulo studied his two remaining cards, as if uncertain which one to play.

"Yes, yes, very amusing," grunted the Abbot. "Come on, play the queen of diamonds. We haven't got all night."

"To see the queen of diamonds, you will have to wait one more trick, I'm afraid," quipped the Italian. "I shall play . . . yes, the ten of hearts."

The Abbot blinked, then leaned over to view Brother Paulo's remaining card, still expecting it to be the diamond queen. A black card, undeniably the king of clubs, stared back at him.

"I think, perhaps, that is making up for the other one," chuckled Brother Paulo.

"I don't think my play can be improved upon," replied the Abbot stiffly. "The odds favoured playing you for the diamond queen at the end."

Brother Paulo thought back over the mistakes the Abbot had made. Since the king of clubs was likely to be with West, he should surely have overtaken ♣ 10 in dummy. He could then have ruffed the clubs good and scored an overtrick. Secondly, there was scarcely room for West to hold a four-card diamond suit. The percentage play in diamonds was king, ace and another, netting an easy twelve tricks.

"Playing with the odds does not always bring its reward," observed the Italian drily.

With a sigh the Abbot reached for his scorepad. "How very true," he said.

4

The Abbot Plays Hide-and-Seek

The sun was streaming into the monastery library where Brother Michael and the Abbot were engrossed in some paperwork.

"I saw a purple fritillary in the allotment this morning, Abbot," said Brother Michael, blowing on a sheet of paper in an attempt to dry the ink.

". . . one hundred and forty-six pounds fifty-nine," muttered the Abbot, ". . . one hundred and . . ."

"Most unusual at this time of year," continued Brother Michael. "I think it was a female, but you can't always tell."

The Abbot rose to his feet. "I had a strange notion I might find some quiet in here while Brother Damien cleaned my study," he said. "Stupid of me. I should have preferred the main pump-room."

Waving aside Brother Michael's apologies, the Abbot swept up his papers and headed back towards his cell. As he passed the senior card-room he glanced inside and was surprised to see a £1 game in progress.

"Playing bridge at this time of the morning?" he exclaimed. "What a disgraceful example to the rest of our brethren. Have you no duties to perform?"

"Yes, this is my last hand," replied Brother Xavier, the monastery barber. "I should have opened shop ten minutes ago."

"Oh well, I might as well sit in for a few deals, I suppose," said the Abbot. "I can't do any work until Brother Damien has finished my study. Why he takes such an age over it, I'll never know."

The Abbot was soon ensconced in the seat vacated by Brother Xavier. This was the first deal:

Love all
Dealer South

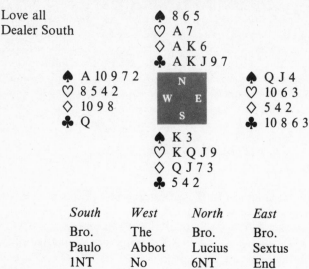

	South	West	North	East
	Bro.	*The*	*Bro.*	*Bro.*
	Paulo	Abbot	Lucius	Sextus
	1NT	No	6NT	End

The Abbot, beginning to regret his decision to join the game, led ◇ 10 against 6NT. Brother Paulo won with the queen and led a low club. The Abbot's queen appeared and dummy's ace won the trick. Brother Paulo paused for thought. If East had the clubs stopped, as seemed possible, then the only chance of an extra trick would be to find the ace of spades onside.

Declarer marked time by cashing his top cards in the red suits. Brother Sextus, sitting East, discarded a low spade and then, perforce, a spade honour. These cards remained:

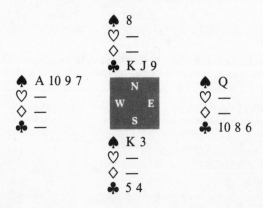

When Brother Paulo crossed to the king of clubs and led a spade, East's queen appeared. From declarer's point of view this card was every bit as welcome as the ace. He followed with a low spade from hand and East was left to lead into dummy's club tenace.

"I don't believe it, partner!" exclaimed the Abbot. "Surely it's obvious to discard the queen and jack of spades?"

"I had to throw the 4 first," replied Brother Sextus bravely, "in case declarer had the king–ten of spades."

"You were obviously going to have to find two discards," persisted the Abbot. "Retaining a spade honour could never gain."

"Perhaps you could have helped me by discarding the ten of spades," suggested Brother Sextus.

"Oh yes, that would be a great idea," replied the Abbot heavily. "I do like to save declarer a guess when he might hold the king-jack. Anyhow, didn't your first discard come before mine?"

The Abbot's humour was not restored when on the next deal he picked up a miserable one-count.

North–South game   ♠ Q 8 2
Dealer West   ♡ K 7 6
                  ♢ 10 7 6 4 2
                  ♣ 10 6

♠ J 10 7 6 3   ♠ 9
♡ 10 9 4   **N**   ♡ J 5 3 2
♢ 8   **W**   **E**   ♢ A K Q J 9 5 3
♣ 8 5 4 2   **S**   ♣ 7

                  ♠ A K 5 4
                  ♡ A Q 8
                  ♢ —
                  ♣ A K Q J 9 3

South	West	North	East
Bro.	The	Bro.	Bro.
Paulo	Abbot	Lucius	Sextus
—	No	No	3NT
6♣	6♢	Double	No
6♠	No	No	No

Over East's gambling 3NT Brother Paulo made the workmanlike call of six clubs. The Abbot could see little defence to this contract, so he opted for the save in six diamonds. North made the obvious double but Brother Paulo was unwilling to assign his magnificent hand to defence. He closed the auction with a splendidly undisciplined call of six spades.

The Abbot led his singleton diamond, which was ruffed by declarer. Brother Paulo continued with the ace of trumps, dropping East's 9, and a low trump. The Abbot hesitated for one fatal moment, then decided to split his honours. Dummy won with the queen and East discarded a diamond.

"You did not double, Abbot?" queried Brother Paulo, giving his superior a playful smile. "Did you think we might run to no-trumps?"

The Abbot looked back stonily. "You're in the dummy," he said.

Brother Paulo cashed four rounds of clubs and three rounds of hearts, ending on the table. These cards remained:

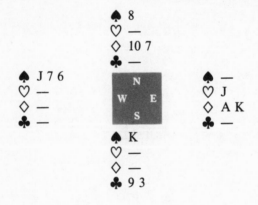

Declarer now ruffed a diamond with the king of spades and led a club from hand. The Abbot was helpless; he could take only one trick.

Brother Sextus totted up the rubber resignedly. What on earth was the Abbot thinking of, splitting his trump honours? If he'd played low smoothly, declarer would never have got it right.

"A good board for us, partner," declared the Abbot. "Seven clubs was quite cold. One round of trumps and a spade ruff sees it home."

"Yes, we were very fortunate," replied Brother Sextus, reaching for his wallet. "Just 23 points away, I make it."

"Ah, there you are, Abbot," said young Brother Damien, poking his head round the cardroom door. "I finished your study ages ago. I never thought of looking for you in here at this time of day."

"Had you found me in the library just ten minutes ago, you would have saved me a considerable sum of money," replied the Abbot severely. "You youngsters have no common sense at all. Where else did you think I'd go to finish my paperwork in peace? The main pump-room?"

5

Brother Damien's Oversight

The Thursday night pairs was well under way when the Abbot and
Brother Lucius arrived at the table occupied by the leading pair from
the novitiate. The Abbot had been having the better of such
encounters in recent weeks and had every intention of extending his
good run. Any novice pair who had the whiff of a good board against
him would spread the story like wildfire. Such was the price of fame,
thought the Abbot, giving a resigned sigh as he pulled back his chair.
This was the first deal:

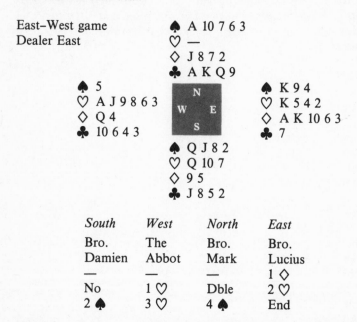

East–West game   ♠ A 10 7 6 3
Dealer East   ♡ —
                 ◊ J 8 7 2
                 ♣ A K Q 9

♠ 5   ♠ K 9 4
♡ A J 9 8 6 3   ♡ K 5 4 2
◊ Q 4   ◊ A K 10 6 3
♣ 10 6 4 3   ♣ 7

                 ♠ Q J 8 2
                 ♡ Q 10 7
                 ◊ 9 5
                 ♣ J 8 5 2

South	West	North	East
Bro.	The	Bro.	Bro.
Damien	Abbot	Mark	Lucius
—	—	—	1 ◊
No	1 ♡	Dble	2 ♡
2 ♠	3 ♡	4 ♠	End

The Abbot led the queen of diamonds against four spades and
continued with another diamond at trick 2. Brother Lucius won with
the king, a mild deception, and returned ◊ 3. Since there was no good
reason for the Abbot to have led the queen from Q 10 x, Brother
Damien ruffed the third round of diamonds high, with the queen.
West discarded a heart.

So far so good, thought Brother Damien. Now, how should he

tackle the trumps? West's failure to overruff marked the king of spades with East. If declarer took a losing finesse of dummy's 10 of trumps, Brother Lucius would certainly fire back another diamond. There would then be an unpleasant guess to make – whether to ruff with the jack or the 8. No, there was no point in taking a finesse that was bound to lose, thought Brother Damien. He crossed to the ace of spades and returned a low spade. Brother Lucius won with the king and led back a third round of trumps. Short of trumps now to dispose of all his losers, declarer was one down.

"Yes, I could have given myself a chance by finessing the 10 of trumps," said Brother Damien. "Rather strange, that, when you know the finesse is going to lose. Still, I don't think I'd have guessed right when another diamond came through. It must be against the odds for the hand with the doubleton diamond to have only one trump."

"How about ruffing a heart at trick 4, then leading a low spade from dummy?" suggested Brother Lucius. "I don't think we can touch you, then."

"That's how it struck me too," confirmed the Abbot.

The scoresheet revealed that going one off in four spades was above average for the young pair. Two East–West pairs had made five hearts doubled and two North–South pairs had been pushed to the five-level in spades.

"Do you think you might have called *four* hearts on the second round, Abbot?" enquired Brother Lucius. "That fitting honour in diamonds was a good card."

"I don't see why I should bid your hand for you," retorted the Abbot. "A rebid of two hearts hardly does justice to your powerful collection."

The post-mortem was interrupted by the arrival of Brother Cameron, a lanky nineteen-year-old with prominent teeth. "Mind if I watch?" he asked, pulling up a chair before anyone could answer.

"Your hair needs cutting," observed the Abbot. "I told you that a couple of days ago."

"Ah, board 16," said Brother Cameron. "I watched that one at another table. What did you do on it?"

"One down in four spades," replied Brother Damien.

"Good board," declared Brother Cameron. "Five hearts is on ice the other way."

"Would you be quiet!" demanded the Abbot. "Those with nothing better to do than kibitz should be like the old-time movies – seen and not heard."

The next board was soon on the table.

Game all
Dealer South

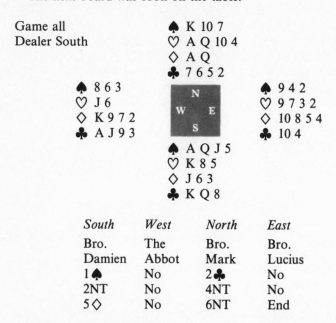

```
                    ♠ K 10 7
                    ♡ A Q 10 4
                    ◇ A Q
                    ♣ 7 6 5 2
  ♠ 8 6 3                          ♠ 9 4 2
  ♡ J 6              N             ♡ 9 7 3 2
  ◇ K 9 7 2       W   E           ◇ 10 8 5 4
  ♣ A J 9 3          S            ♣ 10 4
                    ♠ A Q J 5
                    ♡ K 8 5
                    ◇ J 6 3
                    ♣ K Q 8
```

South	West	North	East
Bro.	The	Bro.	Bro.
Damien	Abbot	Mark	Lucius
1♠	No	2♣	No
2NT	No	4NT	No
5◇	No	6NT	End

Brother Mark could think of no good response to one spade. Two clubs seemed absurd on four to the 7 and two hearts would promise a five-card suit. A jump to 3NT was surely out of the question. If partner held something like ♠ A Q J x x ♡ K x x ◇ K x x x ♣ x, 3NT might fail with twelve tricks available in spades. It seemed like quite a good hand to send to one of the magazine bidding competitions.

Sensing that the Abbot was preparing some unfavourable comment, Brother Mark decided to respond two clubs despite the poor suit. His partner rebid two no-trumps, which they played as forcing, and he raised to four no-trumps. Brother Damien was fairly sure that four no-trumps was a natural call but his ♣ K Q x were looking pretty good opposite partner's suit. There was always the chance that the call was intended as Blackwood anyhow. A few seconds later the young pair were in 6NT.

"I won't embarrass you by asking for an explanation of the bidding," said the Abbot, peering over his glasses. "My lead, is it?"

The Abbot led a low spade, won by dummy's 10. At trick 2 Brother Damien played a club to the king and ace. The Abbot returned another spade, which declarer won in hand. Brother Damien finessed the queen of diamonds successfully and cashed four rounds of hearts, discarding a club. He then returned to hand with the ace of spades and led his last spade in this end-position:

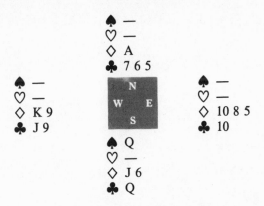

Hoping for the best, the Abbot discarded ♣ 9 but Brother Damien had no difficulty in reading the situation. He cashed the queen of clubs, dropping the jack and 10, then crossed to the diamond ace to enjoy dummy's club winner.

"That sort of thing happens to me time and time again," declared the Abbot. "An absurd auction leading to an even more absurd contract; then the cards lie so kindly that the contract falls into declarer's lap."

Brother Cameron, who had followed the hand with interest, leaned forward. "I may be wrong, Abbot," he said, "but what happens if you hold off your ace of clubs at trick 2?"

The Abbot, pretending not to hear, scribbled something indecipherable on the back of his scorecard.

"I don't think declarer can do it then," persisted Brother Cameron. "In fact he'd probably try leading towards the queen of clubs and go two down."

"Did someone speak?" said the Abbot, turning round fiercely. "I thought I told you to be quiet. No wonder you can't find anyone to partner you if you make gratuitous comments at the end of every hand."

Silence reigned as the players extracted their cards for the last board of the round.

North–South game
Dealer West

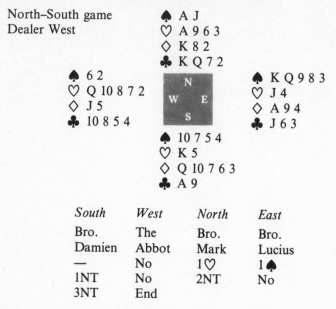

♠ A J
♡ A 9 6 3
◇ K 8 2
♣ K Q 7 2

♠ 6 2
♡ Q 10 8 7 2
◇ J 5
♣ 10 8 5 4

♠ K Q 9 8 3
♡ J 4
◇ A 9 4
♣ J 6 3

♠ 10 7 5 4
♡ K 5
◇ Q 10 7 6 3
♣ A 9

South	*West*	*North*	*East*
Bro.	The	Bro.	Bro.
Damien	Abbot	Mark	Lucius
—	No	1♡	1♠
1NT	No	2NT	No
3NT	End		

Once more the cards lay in the novices' direction. They reached 3NT and the Abbot led ♠ 6.

"Jack, please," said Brother Damien, after a cursory glance at the dummy.

Brother Lucius was not to be rushed with his defence. Studying his own hand and the dummy's in his usual calm manner, he wondered if there was any way for the defenders to come to five tricks. Dummy's ♡ 9 made the prospects in that suit somewhat poor. Neither did it look very attractive to attack diamonds, not from his seat anyhow.

Brother Lucius decided that the spade suit was the defenders' only hope. In that case it was clear that he should allow the table's jack to win the first trick. Then, if the Abbot came in early he would be able to clear the spade suit before the ace of diamonds had been dislodged.

When the jack of spades won the first trick Brother Damien crossed to the ace of clubs and played a diamond to the king. At exactly his normal tempo Brother Lucius followed with the 4.

The young declarer was slightly surprised that Lucius didn't hold the ace of diamonds. Still, a non-vulnerable one spade overcall didn't promise the earth. "Eight of diamonds, please," he called.

The 8 was covered by the 9, 10 and jack. As if by magic, the Abbot was on lead and he still had a spade left. Brother Damien won the spade return with dummy's ace and had little alternative but to press on with diamonds. Brother Lucius produced the ace and cashed three spade tricks to put the game one down.

The two youngsters nodded respectfully in Brother Lucius's direction. They recognised a good defence when they saw it.

"Do we need to explain that one to you?" grunted the Abbot, turning towards Brother Cameron.

"No, it was a great defence, Abbot," came the reply. "When the dummy went down I couldn't see any way the contract could fail."

"Quite so," agreed the Abbot. "It just shows what can be done when two expert defenders are in harness."

"I suppose I should have read the situation and gone up with the queen on the second round of diamonds," said Brother Damien. "Lucius's overcall made it likely that he had the ace of diamonds."

Brother Lucius nodded. "Not only that," he said. "Unless I had a certain card of re-entry I'd be most unlikely to give you a second spade trick. Particularly at pairs."

"He's right," observed Brother Cameron, brushing the Abbot's shoulder as he leaned forward once more. "There was a similar hand in the *Sunday Telegraph* last . . ."

"Be quiet!" commanded the Abbot. "If we ever introduce Vu-Graph into the monastery, I'll bear you in mind as a commentator. Until then, you may consider yourself banned from the senior cardroom."

6

The Penance of Brother James

Brother James, one of the youngest postulants in the monastery, entered the senior card-room and looked around nervously.

"Would you like to join us?" called Brother Lucius from the £1 table. "We're one short."

"No, no. Your game's much too strong for me," replied Brother James, taking the suggestion seriously. "I was hoping to find the Abbot here."

"What an indictment of our esteemed superior!" exclaimed Brother Xavier. "This young fellow would have been quite willing to cut in if the Abbot had been playing."

"No, that's not what I meant at all," replied Brother James, producing a scroll of paper from under his arm. "I had to score last night's duplicate pairs. The Abbot imposed it as a penance when I overslept on Tuesday morning. I missed Matins."

Brother Lucius smiled at the youngster. "Come back in half an hour," he said. "The Abbot should be along by then."

Brother James had scarcely departed when the Abbot made his ponderous entry and the game commenced.

Love all
Dealer North

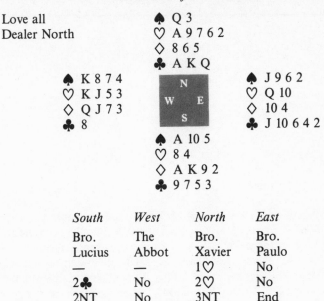

♠ Q 3
♡ A 9 7 6 2
◇ 8 6 5
♣ A K Q

♠ K 8 7 4
♡ K J 5 3
◇ Q J 7 3
♣ 8

♠ J 9 6 2
♡ Q 10
◇ 10 4
♣ J 10 6 4 2

♠ A 10 5
♡ 8 4
◇ A K 9 2
♣ 9 7 5 3

South	West	North	East
Bro.	The	Bro.	Bro.
Lucius	Abbot	Xavier	Paulo
—	—	1♡	No
2♣	No	2♡	No
2NT	No	3NT	End

The Abbot led ◇ 3 against 3NT and East's 10 was taken by the ace. The only realistic prospect was to make something of dummy's hearts, so Brother Lucius ran ♡ 8 to East's 10. A diamond was returned to West's jack. The Abbot had a foreboding that he might come under pressure later, but for the moment he exited safely with his singleton club.

"Brother James was looking for you a few moments ago, Abbot," said Brother Lucius, winning the club in dummy and ducking another heart. "He had the results of last night's pairs with him."

"He was looking for me, you say?" said the Abbot, with a satisfied nod.

East won the second round of hearts and played back a club. Brother Lucius cashed the ace of hearts but the suit failed to break. His next move was to put the Abbot on lead with a heart. This was the end position:

♠ Q 3
♥ 9
♦ 8
♣ Q

♠ K 8 7
♥ —
♦ Q 7
♣ —

♠ J 9 6
♥ —
♦ —
♣ J 10

♠ A 10
♥ —
♦ K 9
♣ 9

When the Abbot exited with ♠ 7 it seemed that Lucius would have to guess the suit correctly. In fact Lucius realised that he could afford to misguess provided West held one or other spade honour. He played low from dummy and captured East's jack with the ace. He then crossed to the queen of clubs and played dummy's last heart, discarding a spade from hand. The Abbot was caught in a simple squeeze. When he discarded a diamond, Brother Lucius claimed the contract.

The Abbot was unimpressed by this commonplace display. "Did Brother James mention any results from last night?" he queried.

"No, he didn't, Abbot," replied Brother Xavier. "But I took down our scores from the travelling score-slips. I made us nearly three tops over."

The cards were soon dealt for the next hand:

North–South game
Dealer East

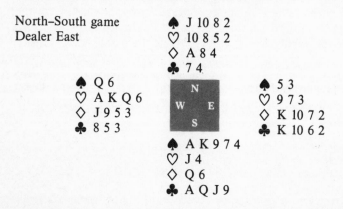

♠ J 10 8 2
♥ 10 8 5 2
♦ A 8 4
♣ 7 4

♠ Q 6
♥ A K Q 6
♦ J 9 5 3
♣ 8 5 3

♠ 5 3
♥ 9 7 3
♦ K 10 7 2
♣ K 10 6 2

♠ A K 9 7 4
♥ J 4
♦ Q 6
♣ A Q J 9

South	West	North	East
Bro.	The	Bro.	Bro.
Lucius	Abbot	Xavier	Paulo
—	—	—	No
1♠	No	2♠	No
4♠	End		

The Abbot cashed the ace–king of hearts against four spades and switched to ◇ 3. When declarer played low from dummy, East won with the king and returned the 2. Brother Lucius overtook the queen of diamonds with the ace and finessed successfully in clubs. He then cashed the black aces, leaving these cards outstanding:

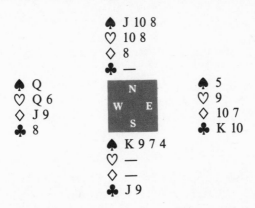

```
              ♠ J 10 8
              ♡ 10 8
              ◇ 8
              ♣ —
♠ Q                        ♠ 5
♡ Q 6          N           ♡ 9
◇ J 9        W   E         ◇ 10 7
♣ 8            S           ♣ K 10
              ♠ K 9 7 4
              ♡ —
              ◇ —
              ♣ J 9
```

The nine of clubs was now ruffed in dummy. Brother Paulo, sitting East, had been following declarer's manoeuvres with interest. Why had Lucius not drawn trumps? It looked as if he had a crucial guess to make in the trump suit. Hoping to induce a miscount, Brother Paulo dropped his king on the third round of clubs.

Brother Lucius paused to assess the evidence. East had played upwards in hearts, so hearts were 4–3. West had switched to ◇ 3 and East had returned the 2, so diamonds appeared to be 4–4. If East had started with ♣ K x x, his shape must be 3–3–4–3. With a fair measure of confidence, Brother Lucius ran the jack of trumps. The Abbot gleefully produced the queen and the game was one down.

"Yes, an excellent combined effort," declared the Abbot. "It was essential for me to switch to the 3 of diamonds to give him a count of the suit. Did you see that, partner?"

"Quite so, Abbot. Well defended," replied Brother Paulo. "Now, I think it is our turn to having some good cards."

Brother Paulo's words were not prophetic. The very next hand found Lucius in game once more.

North–South game
Dealer South

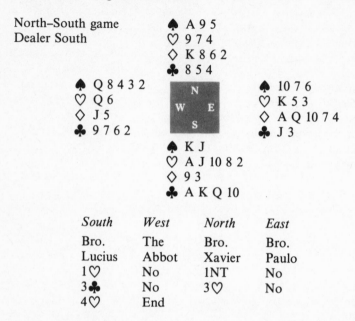

```
                    ♠ A 9 5
                    ♡ 9 7 4
                    ◇ K 8 6 2
                    ♣ 8 5 4
♠ Q 8 4 3 2                        ♠ 10 7 6
♡ Q 6           N                  ♡ K 5 3
◇ J 5        W     E               ◇ A Q 10 7 4
♣ 9 7 6 2          S               ♣ J 3
                    ♠ K J
                    ♡ A J 10 8 2
                    ◇ 9 3
                    ♣ A K Q 10
```

South	West	North	East
Bro.	The	Bro.	Bro.
Lucius	Abbot	Xavier	Paulo
1♡	No	1NT	No
3♣	No	3♡	No
4♡	End		

The Abbot led the jack of diamonds and continued with a second diamond when declarer ducked in dummy. East won with the queen and returned a third round of the suit, declarer ruffing with the jack. The Abbot overruffed with the queen and switched to a spade. Declarer was now easily home. He won the spade switch in dummy and ran ♡ 9. He then repeated the heart finesse before turning his attention to the club suit. When the jack fell on the second round, he was able to draw the last trump and claim the contract.

"Can he do it if you don't overruff, Abbot?" said Brother Paulo. "I think he cannot. There is only one entry to dummy."

"He can always play me for Q x or K x in trumps," replied the Abbot. "Not that difficult, is it? He simply leads a low trump from hand."

"No good. You just duck," replied Brother Paulo. "I win with the king and promote your queen of trumps with another diamond."

[44]

"Overruffing with the queen gains when you hold ♡ 10 8 x," declared the Abbot, after some thought. "Or even ♡ 10 x x, for that matter. Declarer has no reason not to cash the top trumps. Anyhow, I don't seem to have any money with me. I'll have to fetch some from my cell."

The Abbot left the card-room and collided with Brother James in the corridor outside.

"I'm so sorry, Abbot," gasped Brother James, clutching his ribs. "My fault entirely. I've done the scoring for last night's pairs, as you suggested."

"Ah, let's have a look," said the Abbot, unrolling the scoresheet. "What's this? Lucius was two matchpoints ahead of me? Did you remember to subtract Lucius's half-a-top fine for slow play on the last round?"

"I did administer the fine, Abbot," replied Brother James, "but Brother Zac said that one sixth of a top was the normal amount for slow play."

"In straightforward cases, yes," said the Abbot. "But Lucius was still only halfway through the hand when everyone else was leaving the card-room." The Abbot paused, studying the scoresheet suspiciously. "This is all very neat," he observed. "As it was a penance, I thought I told you to do it all with your left hand."

"So I did, Abbot," replied Brother James. "But, actually . . . well, I'm left-handed."

The Abbot rolled up the scoresheet. "That was a despicable evasion on your part," he said. "It'll all have to be done again; this time with your right hand. And don't forget that Lucius should be docked a full half top. Slow play by the senior players is quite inexcusable."

7

The Abbot's Good News

The bell from the outer door sounded and Brother Sextus, the monastery janitor, hobbled across the courtyard. Who could it be, he wondered. An itinerant friar seeking a haven for the night? He pushed open the heavy oak door.

"Hullo. We're here for the bridge match," said a bearded 20-year-old. "We're the Southampton University team."

Brother Sextus peered into the darkness, inspecting the four team members. At the end of the line he could just make out someone with long blonde hair and a pink pullover.

"There must be some mistake," said Brother Sextus. "If your team contains a lady member, I can't let you in. The match should have been arranged for the Dolphin Hotel."

The bearded student laughed. "That's no lady, that's my partner," he replied. "Name of Meecher. Dave Meecher. If there's any dispute about it I'm sure he'd be willing to . . ."

"No, no. Of course not," said Brother Sextus. "Please accept my apologies; the light is poor. Now, come this way,"

The match was soon in progress.

East–West game
Dealer South

	♠ J 9 3	
	♡ A K	
	◇ A K 8 4	
	♣ A K J 10	
♠ K 10 5		♠ 7 6 2
♡ 10 8 6 3	N	♡ Q 5 4 2
◇ 10 2	W E	◇ J 9 7 5
♣ Q 8 5 4	S	♣ 6 3
	♠ A Q 8 4	
	♡ J 9 7	
	◇ Q 6 3	
	♣ 9 7 2	

South	West	North	East
Steve	Bro.	Dave	Bro.
Craggs	Lucius	Meecher	Paulo
No	No	2♣	No
2NT	No	3NT	No
4NT	No	6NT	End

The student team reached 6NT when their North player, for no very good reason, advanced over his partner's 4NT limit bid. Brother Lucius led ♡ 3, won by dummy's king.

Craggs, the blonde-bearded captain of the student team, ran the jack of spades at trick 2. Brother Lucius allowed this card to hold, contributing the 10 from the West seat. Craggs continued with ♠ 9, which was also allowed to win. The young declarer was vaguely surprised to see Brother Lucius produce a second spade at this trick. Did West have a doubleton spade? What a fatuous echo if he did, thought Craggs. And this Lucius character was reputedly the monastery's best player.

"Three of spades," said Craggs, proceeding to finesse the queen.

Brother Lucius won with the bare king and returned another heart, taken in the dummy. Craggs sat back in his chair to re-appraise the situation. He glanced once more at the impassive features of Brother Lucius. Fancy a monk doing that to you, he thought.

Declarer had been deprived of a second entry to hand. To make the contract now he would need to find the club queen onside *and* score a fourth trick in one of the minors. Since he needed to discover which discard to make on the ace of spades, Craggs cashed the ace and king of diamonds before crossing to the queen. Diamonds failed to break, so he discarded dummy's last diamond on the ace of spades. A successful finesse of the jack of clubs gave declarer momentary hope, but when the queen failed to drop on the next two rounds he was one down.

Craggs gave a respectful nod in Brother Lucius's direction. "I was a bit suspicious of that 10 of spades," he said. "But . . . well, some people do play high–low with a doubleton, regardless."

Brother Lucius smiled back. "True," he said. "It was difficult for you."

Unlike the Abbot, Brother Lucius would never point out an opponent's mistake. It occurred to him, though, that declarer should have played a low spade to the 8 on the second round of the suit. If this had been ducked, declarer could have taken a club finesse. He could then have returned to the queen of diamonds and repeated the club finesse. With twelve tricks in the bag he would obviously have spurned a further spade finesse and ended with thirteen tricks when the bare king fell offside.

"I'm feeling rather cold in here, actually," said Dave Meecher, rubbing the arms of his pink pullover. "No chance of some heat, is there?"

"Unfortunately, no," replied Brother Paulo. "Everywhere is cold here. I noticed it most strongly when I first came from Italy."

"You'll be all right in the second half," observed Brother Lucius, sorting his cards for the next deal. "At this time of year the Abbot always keeps a fire going in his study."

"I thought it was the home team that normally changed seats at half-time," said Meecher.

"Not in this establishment," replied Brother Lucius. "Not from October to April, anyway."

One floor above them, the Abbot had just reached a vulnerable heart slam.

Game all
Dealer South

	♠ —	
	♡ K 7 5 3	
	◇ A K Q 8	
	♣ A J 7 6 5	
♠ 10 4 3		♠ Q J 8 5
♡ 6	N	♡ J 9 8 2
◇ J 10 9 6 3	W E	◇ 7 4 2
♣ K 10 9 2	S	♣ Q 4
	♠ A K 9 7 6 2	
	♡ A Q 10 4	
	◇ 5	
	♣ 8 3	

South	West	North	East
The	Doug	Bro.	Mark
Abbot	Spitzer	Xavier	Bachman
1♠	No	2♣	No
2♡	No	3◇	No
3♠	No	6♡	End

If the Abbot had rebid his hearts over three diamonds, Brother Xavier was planning to jump to 5NT, Josephine. When the Abbot rebid in spades, implying only four hearts, Brother Xavier closed the auction with a leap to six hearts.

The jack of diamonds lead was won in the dummy and the Abbot continued with a trump to the queen. He then cashed the top two spades and ruffed a spade, everyone following. The lead was in dummy and these cards were still at large:

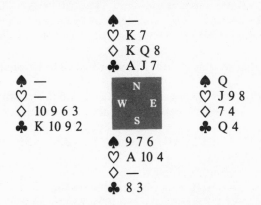

```
              ♠ —
              ♡ K 7
              ◇ K Q 8
              ♣ A J 7
  ♠ —                        ♠ Q
  ♡ —                        ♡ J 9 8
  ◇ 10 9 6 3                 ◇ 7 4
  ♣ K 10 9 2                 ♣ Q 4
              ♠ 9 7 6
              ♡ A 10 4
              ◇ —
              ♣ 8 3
```

The Abbot scratched his ear thoughtfully. If he played king and another trump he would lose control of the hand if either defender had started with four trumps. (He could pick up ♡ J 9 8 with East but would still be a trick short.) What could be done? It seemed to the Abbot that he could improve his chances by making the odd-looking play of a trump to the ace. That would still allow the contract to be made if trumps were 3–2 and would give him some extra chances otherwise.

After a trump to the ace, on which West showed out, the Abbot crossed back to dummy with the ace of clubs. He then cashed the king and queen of diamonds, discarding a club, and ruffed a club in hand. Finally he ruffed a spade with dummy's king and led a club towards his bare 10 of trumps. East, with ♡ J 9 remaining, was powerless to prevent the Abbot scoring a twelfth trick.

"Make a note of the hand for my next monastery bulletin, will you," instructed the Abbot, sitting back triumphantly in his chair. "A *coup en passant*, if I'm not mistaken."

Not long afterwards the monastery team were busy comparing scores for the first half. They soon came to the no-trump hand.

"Plus 490," said the Abbot with a slight look of concern.

"Plus 50," said Brother Lucius. "They were one down in 6NT."

"Really?" exclaimed the Abbot. "How pathetic. There were twelve on top, weren't there?"

A few moments later they came to the heart slam.

"Well, we have good news and bad news for you on this one," said the Abbot, a mischievous glint in his eye. "The bad news is that we bid the slam." He paused to let his words sink in. "The good news is that I managed to find a way home, despite the bad trump break. Plus 980!"

"Oh, well played, Abbot," said Brother Lucius, not sounding very impressed.

"Yes, a cross-ruff ending in a *coup en passant*," continued the Abbot. "Not a sequence of plays that would occur to a mere student, I fancy."

"Quite so," replied Brother Lucius. "I'm afraid they made the grand against us."

The Abbot blinked in disbelief.

"Seemed fairly straightforward," continued Brother Lucius. "He won the diamond lead, took one round of trumps with the queen, cashed five more side suit winners and crossruffed the remainder."

"Ah, I see," said Brother Xavier. "He ruffed three spades in the dummy, you mean."

"That's right," replied Brother Lucius. "Two low ruffs and then a master spade ruffed with the king."

"Easy enough if you're actually in seven," observed the Abbot, recovering his composure. He turned towards Brother Xavier. "Bit feeble jumping straight to six, wasn't it?" he said. "We had thirteen tricks on top."

PART II

Interlude in Africa

8

Chief Krazulah's Contribution

The Bozwambi team's adventures in the African Championship were fading into past memory. They had found it difficult to adjust themselves to playing in the local league again and after four matches were occupying only a disappointing third position. Their match against the league leaders, the Hadjahuk Headshrinkers, had therefore assumed considerable importance. Before the game started, the two teams gathered in Brother Tobias's hut to enjoy some scented tea, a Bozwambi speciality made from mulberry leaves.

"How did your team come by its interesting name?" said Brother Tobias, eyeing the feather-bedecked opposing captain. "Presumably the term 'Headshrinkers' is of historical significance only?"

"Not at all," replied Chief Krazulah solemnly. "We like to keepin' de old skills alive."

Brother Tobias took a sip of tea and looked uncertainly at the Chieftain. "Not on human beings, I trust," he said, with a short laugh. "You must mean you practise on small monkeys."

"Yes, indeed," replied the Chieftain, "if you includin' our neighbours de Bahuku tribe in dat category." He paused to shake the tea leaves from his cup onto Brother Tobias's best carpet. "We killin' lots of Bahuku all de time," he continued. "Also few stupid white Bwanas who wanderin' into our territory."

"Don't mention this to my colleague, Brother Luke," said Brother Tobias. 'He's very straight-laced. Knowing him, he'd take it all seriously."

The two teams were soon facing each other at the card table.

North–South game
Dealer South

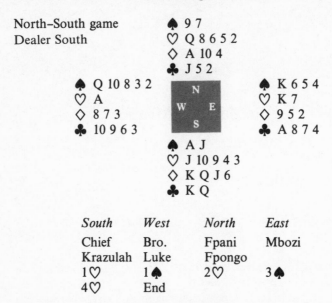

```
                    ♠ 9 7
                    ♡ Q 8 6 5 2
                    ◇ A 10 4
                    ♣ J 5 2
♠ Q 10 8 3 2                        ♠ K 6 5 4
♡ A                N                ♡ K 7
◇ 8 7 3        W       E            ◇ 9 5 2
♣ 10 9 6 3         S               ♣ A 8 7 4
                    ♠ A J
                    ♡ J 10 9 4 3
                    ◇ K Q J 6
                    ♣ K Q
```

South	West	North	East
Chief	Bro.	Fpani	Mbozi
Krazulah	Luke	Fpongo	
1♡	1♠	2♡	3♠
4♡	End		

Aware that the vulnerable opponents might be trying to bump them into a phantom sacrifice, Brother Luke and Mbozi let the bidding die in four hearts. A low spade was led to the king and ace, and Chief Krazulah found himself staring at four seemingly unavoidable losers. Hoping to crash the defenders' trump honours, he crossed to the ace of diamonds and led the queen of hearts.

Mbozi was not to be tempted. Covering with the king would gain only if declarer's trumps were as feeble as A 10 x x. It was much more likely that declarer had something like A J 10 x x x and no intention of running the queen. Mbozi played low and the trick was won by West's ace. Brother Luke cashed a spade trick and the game eventually went one down.

"Why you not coverin' de trump queen?" said Chief Krazulah accusingly. "Seems like you knowin' partner had de bare ace."

Mbozi gave the Chieftain a sullen glance. "What you so worried about?" he said. "You thinkin' your East player's gonna coverin' de queen?"

Not long afterwards the board was replayed in the other hut.

Chief Krazulah's Contribution

South	West	North	East
Witch-doctor	Kahanga	Bro. Tobias	Obu
1♡	No	2♡	No
4♡	End		

Once more a spade was led to the king and ace. The Witchdoctor inspected the dummy thoughtfully. What was the best chance to tempt the defenders into crashing their trump honours? Suddenly it hit him. There was a genuine chance of making the contract. He played three rounds of diamonds, all following, then led a fourth round, discarding dummy's spade loser. It made no difference which defender ruffed. Declarer could lose only two trump tricks and a club.

"I's payin' you compliment with dat line of play," the Witchdoctor informed his opponents. "Against couple of banana pickers I mos' probably try to crashin' de trump honours."

Back in the other hut Chief Krazulah was sorting through an impressive 19-count.

Love all
Dealer South

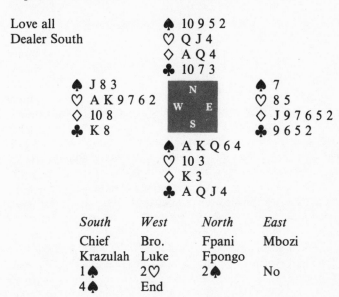

```
            ♠ 10 9 5 2
            ♡ Q J 4
            ◇ A Q 4
            ♣ 10 7 3
♠ J 8 3                    ♠ 7
♡ A K 9 7 6 2      N       ♡ 8 5
◇ 10 8          W     E    ◇ J 9 7 6 5 2
♣ K 8              S       ♣ 9 6 5 2
            ♠ A K Q 6 4
            ♡ 10 3
            ◇ K 3
            ♣ A Q J 4
```

South	West	North	East
Chief Krazulah	Bro. Luke	Fpani Fpongo	Mbozi
1♠	2♡	2♠	No
4♠	End		

Brother Luke led the ace of hearts against four spades, drawing the 4, 8 and 10. Since his partner would not have played the 8 from ♡ 8 5 3, Brother Luke was not put off by the Chieftain's false card. He continued with the king of hearts, followed by a third round of the suit. East ruffed with the 7 and was delighted to see this modest card force declarer's queen.

Chief Krazulah cashed the trump ace and discovered, to his annoyance, that he now had a trump loser. He continued with the ace of trumps and three rounds of diamonds, discarding a club.

Brother Luke declined to ruff this trick, but was thrown in with the jack of trumps anyway on the next trick. Sitting West, he was on lead in this end position:

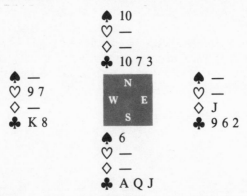

```
                    ♠ 10
                    ♡ —
                    ◇ —
                    ♣ 10 7 3
    ♠ —                               ♠ —
    ♡ 9 7           N                 ♡ —
    ◇ —          W     E              ◇ J
    ♣ K 8           S                 ♣ 9 6 2
                    ♠ 6
                    ♡ —
                    ◇ —
                    ♣ A Q J
```

Since a heart return would give a ruff-and-discard, Brother Luke exited with ♣ 8, won by declarer's jack. Chief Krazulah eyed Brother Luke suspiciously, then paused to consider the situation. Surely if West held ♣ K 8 he would have exited with a heart, realising that he would still come to a club trick. If West held ♣ 8 x, on the other hand, a ruff-and-discard might well give declarer the contract.

Convinced by this defence that the king of clubs must be onside, Chief Krazulah crossed to ♠ 10 and finessed the queen of clubs. Brother Luke produced the club king and cashed a winning heart.

Mbozi looked across the table in disbelief. "You gotta wire loose, Bwana?" he exclaimed. "You gave him chance to makin' it! Why you not leadin' heart and give ruff-discard? You still mus' makin' a club."

"Yes, but that's only one off," replied a beaming Brother Luke. "We got it two off."

At half-time the Bozwambi team led by 25 IMPs. The two teams ceased hostilities to enjoy a barbecue prepared by the Bozwambi womenfolk. The Hadjahuk Chieftain reached into a camel-skin travel bag he had brought with him and extracted a paper-wrapped package which he gave to one of the women cooking the food.

"What was that?" mumbled Brother Tobias, who was already taking advantage of some barbecued jungle chicken legs.

"Just a small contribution to de festivities," replied Chief Krazulah. "Dey not takin' long to cook. I hope you likin' de flavour."

"Yes, but what are they?" persisted Brother Tobias. "Some local speciality of yours?"

"You might sayin' so, I suppose," replied the Chieftain, chuckling to himself. "We callin' 'em Bahuku-burgers."

The two teams had done full justice to the fare provided when the match restarted.

"You feelin' all right, Bwana?" asked Mbozi, noticing that Brother Luke looked somewhat off colour.

"I'd never felt better until a couple of minutes ago," replied Brother Luke. "Then I overheard Chief Krazulah giving the Witchdoctor the recipe for those meat-balls we were just eating."

"Don't worry, Bwana," said Mbozi. "First time always bit strange. You soon gettin' used to eatin' it."

"I wouldn't take another morsel if St. Peter himself requested it," replied Brother Luke. "Now, who dealt this one?"

Love all
Dealer North

	♠ 7 2	
	♡ 6 5	
	◇ A 10 8 6 4	
	♣ A K Q 4	

♠ J 9 3		♠ Q 5
♡ A Q 10 2	N	♡ J 8 7 3
◇ J 5	W E	◇ K Q 7 2
♣ J 10 9 7	S	♣ 6 5 2

	♠ A K 10 8 6 4	
	♡ K 9 4	
	◇ 9 3	
	♣ 8 3	

South	*West*	*North*	*East*
Kahanga	Bro. Luke	Obu	Mbozi
—	—	1 ◇	No
1 ♠	No	2 ♣	No
3 ♠	No	4 ♠	End

[55]

Against four spades Brother Luke led the jack of clubs, won in the dummy. The pot-bellied Kahanga played a heart to the king and ace, and Brother Luke switched to a trump. East's queen forced the ace and declarer re-entered dummy with a club for another heart lead.

Mbozi, in one of his sharper moods, went in with the jack of hearts. He was then able to lead a trump through declarer's K 10, putting the game one down. Declarer eventually lost three heart tricks and a trump.

Obu shook his head. "You missin' clever play on dat one," he informed his partner.

Kahanga glared across the table, indicating with a wave of the hand that the next board should be brought into position.

"You should playin' a heart to de 9 on first round," continued Obu. "West can't leadin' trumps twice from his side without givin' up trump trick."

Brother Luke nodded. "It's a better line, you're quite right," he said. "But can't I stop you by switching to diamonds when I win the first heart? You have to cash two more clubs to discard your diamond and now you're exposed to an uppercut when I win the second heart. I lead a fourth round of clubs and my partner ruffs with the queen."

"Dat's jus' what I was thinkin'," declared Kahanga. "Didn't you spottin' dat, Obu?"

Meanwhile, in the other hut the Witchdoctor had just reached a difficult spade game.

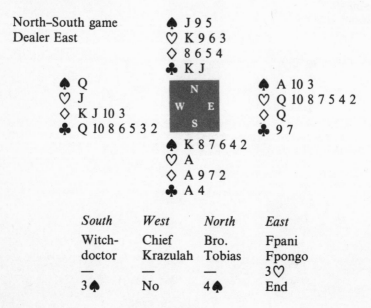

North–South game
Dealer East

		♠ J 9 5	
		♡ K 9 6 3	
		◇ 8 6 5 4	
		♣ K J	
♠ Q			♠ A 10 3
♡ J			♡ Q 10 8 7 5 4 2
◇ K J 10 3			◇ Q
♣ Q 10 8 6 5 3 2			♣ 9 7
		♠ K 8 7 6 4 2	
		♡ A	
		◇ A 9 7 2	
		♣ A 4	

South	West	North	East
Witch-	Chief	Bro.	Fpani
doctor	Krazulah	Tobias	Fpongo
—	—	—	3 ♡
3 ♠	No	4 ♠	End

Chief Krazulah brushed a couple of flies off his gold-embroidered raiment and led the jack of hearts against four spades. The Witchdoctor won with the ace and crossed to the king of clubs for a trump lead. East played low and declarer's king drew the queen from West.

The Witchdoctor paused for thought, picking some remnants of the barbecue from his teeth. It seemed that he had two trump losers. How could he possibly avoid two diamond losers to go with them? It took him just a moment to see the solution. East was 3–7 in the majors. Was it too much to ask that he should hold one diamond and two clubs?

The Witchdoctor cashed the ace of clubs and the ace of diamonds, then exited in trumps. East took his two trump winners but had only hearts remaining. When he returned the queen of hearts the Witchdoctor simply discarded a diamond. East had to continue with a further heart into dummy's K 9 tenace, allowing the Witchdoctor to discard his remaining two diamonds.

"Hah! Should gettin' nice swing on dat one!" exclaimed the Witchdoctor modestly.

"Yes, indeed," agreed Brother Tobias. "Not many people would find the raise to game on my limited values. One of my better efforts."

The next board was soon on the table.

Game all
Dealer South

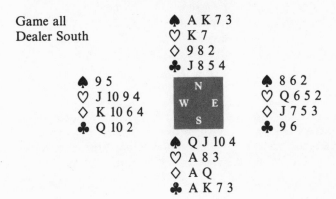

♠ A K 7 3
♡ K 7
◇ 9 8 2
♣ J 8 5 4

♠ 9 5
♡ J 10 9 4
◇ K 10 6 4
♣ Q 10 2

♠ 8 6 2
♡ Q 6 5 2
◇ J 7 5 3
♣ 9 6

♠ Q J 10 4
♡ A 8 3
◇ A Q
♣ A K 7 3

South	West	North	East
Witch-	Chief	Bro.	Fpani
doctor	Krazulah	Tobias	Fpongo
2NT	No	3♣	No
3♠	No	5♠	No
6♠	End		

Chief Krazulah led the jack of hearts against six spades and the Witchdoctor scanned the dummy that Brother Tobias had laid out. There were insufficient trumps for a standard elimination play but perhaps he could achieve a partial elimination.

The Witchdoctor won the heart lead in dummy and took just two rounds of trumps, the queen and the jack. He then ruffed his heart loser and played on clubs. The third round of clubs was led in this end position:

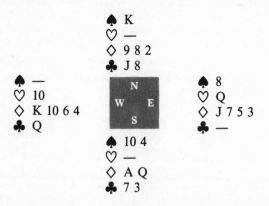

```
                    ♠ K
                    ♡ —
                    ◇ 9 8 2
                    ♣ J 8
        ♠ —                        ♠ 8
        ♡ 10            N          ♡ Q
        ◇ K 10 6 4   W   E         ◇ J 7 5 3
        ♣ Q             S          ♣ —
                    ♠ 10 4
                    ♡ —
                    ◇ A Q
                    ♣ 7 3
```

West won with the queen of clubs and found he was endplayed. A heart would obviously give a ruff-and-discard so he tried a diamond. The Witchdoctor won with the queen and claimed the contract.

Chuckling openly at this success, he turned towards Chief Krazulah in the West seat. "Did you havin' de last trump?" he enquired.

"You tryin' to insultin' me?" cried the Chieftain, producing a dagger from his waistband. "You thinkin' I would exit with diamond if I had trump left?"

"No, mos' stupid of me," replied the Witchdoctor, eyeing the blade with alarm. "But if your partner havin' de last trump, why he not ruffin' your club queen and puttin' a diamond through?"

Fpani Fpongo jerked in his seat as the Chieftain turned his cobra-like eyes upon him.

"Why you not findin' dat defence?" demanded the Chieftain. "You better improvin' your play pretty sharpish or I's gonna makin' pound or two of Fpongo-burgers tonight."

The Chieftain sat back in this chair and gave an imperious sniff. "Mind you," he said. "If you tastin' anything like as bad as you playin', nobody would wantin' to eat any of 'em."

9

The Katangi Massacre Mixed Pairs

The Zbolwumba tribe were holding a Gala Mixed Pairs event to celebrate the fiftieth anniversary of their infamous victory at the Battle of Katangi. Joining in the spirit of the event, the Bozwambi tribe had entered two strong pairs. The Witchdoctor had persuaded Mrs. Okoku to play with him and Brother Tobias was partnered by the Parrot. After a long wait in the hot sun Brother Tobias reached the front of the queue waiting to pay their entrance money.

"What's de name?" barked the Zbolwumba warrior who was taking the entries.

Brother Tobias was annoyed not to be recognised. "You must be new to these parts," he said. "I am Brother Tobias, captain of the team that represented Upper Bhumpopo in the recent African Championships."

The warrior gave him a look of appraisal. "Ah yes, I rememberin' now," he said. "You butcherin' four spade contract on de last hand. I readin' about it in Bhumpopo Bridge Magazine. If you exitin' with fourth round of . . ."

"Do you want our money or don't you?" interrupted Brother Tobias.

"Who's your partner?" asked the warrior, writing busily on the entry sheet.

Brother Tobias gave an impatient sigh. "I'm not in the habit of walking round with a parrot on my shoulder," he said. "This is my partner. Her name is Elspeth."

"Don' lookin' like a female parrot to me," said the warrior, reaching a large hand towards the Parrot. "Let me have a look . . . aargh!"

"Serves you right," said Brother Tobias, tossing some coins on to the table.

As was customary except in the rainy season, the event was held in the open air. Some twenty-five tables had been laid out in the clearing in front of the chieftain's hut.

North–South game
Dealer East

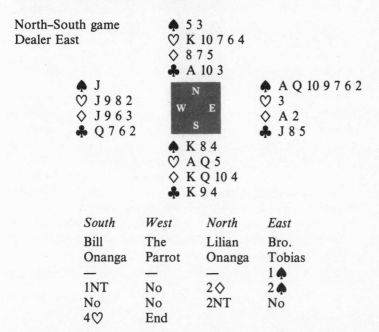

♠ 5 3
♡ K 10 7 6 4
◇ 8 7 5
♣ A 10 3

♠ J
♡ J 9 8 2
◇ J 9 6 3
♣ Q 7 6 2

♠ A Q 10 9 7 6 2
♡ 3
◇ A 2
♣ J 8 5

♠ K 8 4
♡ A Q 5
◇ K Q 10 4
♣ K 9 4

South	West	North	East
Bill	The	Lilian	Bro.
Onanga	Parrot	Onanga	Tobias
—	—	—	1♠
1NT	No	2◇	2♠
No	No	2NT	No
4♡	End		

After Brother Tobias had opened one spade, the Onangas reached four hearts via a transfer sequence. The Parrot led the jack of spades and Brother Tobias won with the ace. The queen of spades return was covered and ruffed and the Parrot returned a low diamond to the ace.

Not giving the matter much thought, Brother Tobias returned ◇ 2. Mr. Onanga won with the king and cashed the ace-queen of trumps. He followed this with the key play of cashing the diamond queen. Although there was still a trump out, there was little risk attached to this play. The queen of diamonds would be ruffed only if East held 7–1–4–1 distribution and West had falsecarded from ◇ 6 3.

East showed out on the third round of diamonds and declarer proceeded to run dummy's trump suit. The last heart was led in this end position:

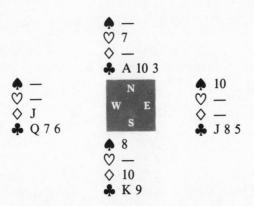

Each defender in turn had to release a club, so declarer scored three club tricks to make the contract exactly. All eyes turned to the Parrot who was hopping up and down in agitated fashion.

"What's the matter with you?" said Brother Tobias. "Have you never seen a double squeeze before?"

"Skrwark!" replied the Parrot, rocking from one claw to the other.

"Parrot-bird quite right," observed Bill Onanga. "You could beatin' de squeeze by returnin' a spade instead of a diamond."

Brother Tobias was somewhat amused at this. "That may be," he said, "But what can a mere parrot know about breaking up squeezes?"

"Kill the menace!" shrieked the Parrot. "Spade back kill the menace. What a silly boy!"

"Be quiet, for heaven's sake," admonished Brother Tobias. "They'll hear you at the next table."

Towards the end of the first session Brother Tobias and the Parrot arrived at the Witchdoctor's table. This was the first board they played:

East–West game
Dealer South

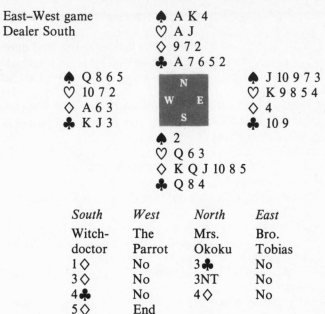

♠ A K 4
♡ A J
◇ 9 7 2
♣ A 7 6 5 2

♠ Q 8 6 5
♡ 10 7 2
◇ A 6 3
♣ K J 3

♠ J 10 9 7 3
♡ K 9 8 5 4
◇ 4
♣ 10 9

♠ 2
♡ Q 6 3
◇ K Q J 10 8 5
♣ Q 8 4

South	West	North	East
Witch-	The	Mrs.	Bro.
doctor	Parrot	Okoku	Tobias
1◇	No	3♣	No
3◇	No	3NT	No
4♣	No	4◇	No
5◇	End		

Mrs. Okoku's steely expression confirmed that she had little to spare for her jump shift. The Witchdoctor therefore restrained himself from bidding a slam. The Parrot led ♠5 and the Witchdoctor made the strange-looking play of ducking in the dummy. Brother Tobias, sitting East, won with the 9 and returned ♣10, covered by the queen, king and ace.

Muttering to himself, the Witchdoctor discarded two clubs on the top spades and ruffed a club in hand with the trump king. When his next lead of the queen of trumps was ducked by West, he continued with the 5 of trumps. The Parrot ducked again and dummy's 7 won the trick. The Witchdoctor now ruffed the clubs good and exited in trumps, claiming the contract.

"What a lead!" complained Brother Tobias, moving swiftly onto the attack. "Surely a heart lead stands out a mile on that bidding?"

The Parrot blinked, trying desperately to recall what the bidding had been.

The Witchdoctor reached for the travelling score sheet. "Hah! We gettin' de only plus-score in de house," he announced. "Three no-trumps, five clubs and five diamonds goin' down all over de place."

"Yes, well, the Parrot wasn't on lead at the other tables," explained Brother Tobias.

"Where was de 3 of spades?" demanded the Witchdoctor, turning his yellow eyes in Brother Tobias's direction. "You havin' it?"

Brother Tobias thumbed through his cards. "Apparently I did," he said. "So what?"

"If you's playin' it at trick one," the Witchdoctor informed him, "your partner's 5 winnin' de trick. He mos' probably switchin' to hearts and killin' de contract."

"Obvious switch, obvious switch," squawked the Parrot. "I couldn't *understand* it when you overtook my card."

Brother Tobias reached for the next board with as much dignity as his bulk would permit. "I'll try not to make the same mistake next time," he said.

The event was well into its second session when a loud voice came from the far side of the jungle clearing. "Results for de first session now bein' posted on tree by de great chieftain's hut," it announced.

"Fly over and see how we did, will you, while I play this hand," said Brother Tobias.

The Parrot took off in the direction of the chieftain's hut, looking pointedly at the sky to escape any suggestion that he was peeking at the cards below.

Brother Tobias had just finished playing the hand when the Parrot swooped back onto his perch. "No good! No good!" he screeched. "Fifty-two dot one percent."

"Point one, not dot one," replied Brother Tobias. "Anyhow that can't be right. I made us at least two tops over." Taking out his card for the first session, he ran a finger down his estimated scores. "Yes, that must be wrong. I'll have to check that later. How are the others doing?"

"Okoku woman and Witchdoctor lying second," replied the Parrot sourly. "Sixty-two dot four percent."

The elderly West player drew polite attention to the fact that another board remained to be played. Once more Brother Tobias ended as declarer.

Love all
Dealer South

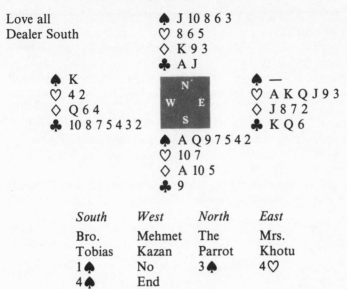

♠ J 10 8 6 3
♡ 8 6 5
◇ K 9 3
♣ A J

♠ K
♡ 4 2
◇ Q 6 4
♣ 10 8 7 5 4 3 2

♠ —
♡ A K Q J 9 3
◇ J 8 7 2
♣ K Q 6

♠ A Q 9 7 5 4 2
♡ 10 7
◇ A 10 5
♣ 9

South	West	North	East
Bro.	Mehmet	The	Mrs.
Tobias	Kazan	Parrot	Khotu
1♠	No	3♠	4♡
4♠	End		

Mehmet Kazan was not one to ignore his partner's suit, even in a mixed pairs. Tapping the ash off his cheroot, he led ♡ 4. Mrs. Khotu cashed two winners in the suit and led a third heart.

Since the king was the only outstanding trump, Brother Tobias decided to ruff the trick with the 2. He chuckled inwardly. That'll be amusing, he thought, if West shows out but can't overruff the 2 of trumps.

Unfortunately for declarer, West did produce the king of trumps. When he exited safely in clubs, there was only a slim chance left of making the contract. Brother Tobias ran the trump suit, keeping ◇ K 9 and ♣ J in dummy and ◇ A 10 5 in hand. There was no squeeze. West won the last trick with the queen of diamonds and the contract was one down.

The Parrot shifted from one claw to the other, clicking his beak disapprovingly.

"What are you going on about?" said Brother Tobias. "Do you really expect me to pass four hearts when I have a seven-card spade suit? Anyhow, we need to find the club ruff to beat four hearts."

"Four spades cold! Four spades cold!" shrieked the Parrot, jabbing at the travelling score-sheet with his beak. "Yes, three pairs made it. Must ruff heart with ace of trumps."

Brother Tobias smiled graciously at the opponents. "I apologise for my partner's ramblings," he said. "But, of course, we must make allowance for the fact that . . ." he lowered his voice to a whisper, "well, he's only a parrot."

"He's right, though, isn't he?" replied Mehmet Kazan. "If you ruff high, eliminate clubs and exit to my king of trumps, I have to open the diamond suit."

Brother Tobias blinked. Then, pretending not to have heard the observation, he snatched the scoresheet from the Parrot's grasp. "I'll fill that in," he said. "No-one can make head or tail of your handwriting, you know that."

The last round of the event found the Parrot and Brother Tobias at the table of Mr. and Mrs. Nfashu. This was the final board:

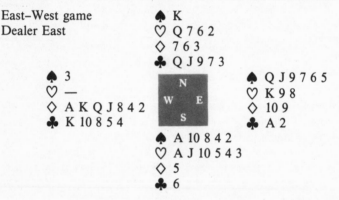

East–West game
Dealer East

```
              ♠ K
              ♡ Q 7 6 2
              ◇ 7 6 3
              ♣ Q J 9 7 3
♠ 3                              ♠ Q J 9 7 6 5
♡ —           N                  ♡ K 9 8
◇ A K Q J 8 4 2   W   E          ◇ 10 9
♣ K 10 8 5 4      S              ♣ A 2
              ♠ A 10 8 4 2
              ♡ A J 10 5 4 3
              ◇ 5
              ♣ 6
```

"Ssss . . . STOP!" screeched the Parrot, who was first to speak in the East seat. "Two diamonds!"

"Is dat Acol?" enquired the heavily-beaded Mrs. Nfashu, sitting South.

"My partner favours a rather complex version of the multi-coloured two diamonds," replied Brother Tobias. "It could be various strong hands or a weak two in one of the majors."

"Which major would dat be?" asked Mrs. Nfashu, fingering through her own splendid collection in that department.

"To discover that, I must bid two no-trumps," replied Brother Tobias.

"Yeah, but what if I wantin' to know?" retorted Mrs. Nfashu. "Don' seem fair you can findin' out an' I can't."

Mrs. Nfashu, fixing one disgruntled eye on Brother Tobias and the other on the Parrot, eventually decided to pass. The following auction ensued:

South	West	North	East
Mrs.	Bro.	Mr.	The
Nfashu	Tobias	Nfashu	Parrot
—	—	—	2◇
No	3◇	No	3♠
4♡	5◇	5♡	Dble
End			

Brother Tobias led the ace of diamonds against five hearts doubled and continued with a second high diamond. Mrs. Nfashu ruffed in hand, crossed to the spade king and led the queen of clubs.

The Parrot won with the ace and inspected the line of cards in his wooden card-holder. What was the best return? If he played back a trump, declarer would finesse the 10 and cash the spade ace. Five black-suit ruffs would then leave her on table with just the ace and jack of hearts remaining in hand. An easy make.

There could be no point in a spade return, so the Parrot eventually tossed a club on the table. Mrs. Nfashu ruffed the club, ruffed a spade and ruffed a diamond, East showing out. She then cashed the spade ace and ruffed a spade in the dummy. This was the end position:

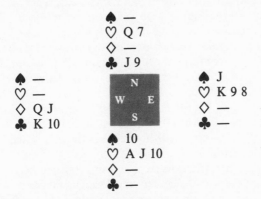

Mrs. Nfashu led ♡ 7 to the 10 and ruffed her last spade with dummy's queen. Exposing her last two cards, the ace and jack of hearts, she now claimed the contract.

"Lead a trump! Lead a trump!" exclaimed the Parrot, hopping up and down on his perch.

"The situation called for a trump lead, I agree," replied Brother Tobias. "Unfortunately I didn't have one."

"Then lead a low diamond and let *me* lead a trump!" screeched the

Parrot, as if addressing a sub-moron.

"Dat's right," agreed Mr. Nfashu. "Then Parrot-bird can leadin' another round of trumps when he gettin' in with de ace of clubs."

Mrs. Nfashu nodded her agreement. "It's in all de books," she said. "Underleadin' de A K Q J when you havin' a void in another suit."

"Not when the void is in trumps," replied an exasperated Brother Tobias.

A large crowd soon gathered round the Zbolwumba chieftain's hut, waiting for the results to be announced. The Witchdoctor and Mrs. Okoku edged their way towards Brother Tobias, who was keeping a low profile.

"Ah, there you are, Bwana!" said the Witchdoctor. "You and Parrot-Bird havin' a good second session?"

"I assume from your manner that you did well yourselves," replied Brother Tobias. "As it happens, the Parrot and I did not have the best of fortune. The event will be a valuable experience for him. Er . . . for her, I mean."

The crowd stirred as the magnificently bedecked Zbolwumba chieftain appeared, result sheet in hand.

"Dis event has bin mos' outstandin' success," he announced. "I would particularly like to congratulatin' myself and team of helpers for de excellent organisation." There was a burst of applause, led by the chieftain himself.

"Dis event commemoratin' our mos' glorious massacre of de Katangi tribe," continued the chieftain, "in which I myself participatin' to no small extent when jus' young warrior." He paused for another round of applause. "And now I tellin' you de two pairs who takin' home de big prizes. In second place are my good friends Mehmet Kazan and Gloria Khotu from Umbala village."

Brother Tobias clapped half-heartedly as the pair walked forward to claim their prizes.

"And in first place, visitors from our mos' valued neighbours, de Bozwambi tribe, are Mrs. Okoku and Dr. Mhemhazzah!"

There was an angry murmuring from some of the Zbolwumba warriors and Brother Tobias thought it wise to defuse the situation. "Mixed pairs events are always a lottery," he announced loudly.

The crowd soon began to disperse. Brother Tobias turned to the Parrot, who was back on his shoulder once more. "By the way," he said, lowering his voice, "are you really a female parrot?"

With a seductive fluttering of the eyelids, the Parrot bent down and pecked Brother Tobias affectionately on the cheek. "Whatever gave you that idea, ducky?" he said.

10

The Sun God's Intervention

The Parrot's reputation had spread far and wide. Dr. Rutter, leader of an ornithological expedition to the Sudan, had flown over 200 miles by helicopter so he could study the Parrot's performance in the Bozwambi rubber bridge final. A large number of kibitzers were expected, so the final was to be played in the open air.

"You gonna watchin' de final, Bwana?" said Mjubu to Brother Luke. "Need to gettin' there early for good view."

"No, I've far more important things to do," replied Brother Luke, who had been in a tetchy mood ever since losing unexpectedly in the quarter finals. "Just think. If you hadn't overstretched to that diamond slam, we might have reached the final ourselves."

Mjubu shrugged his shoulders and walked away. "Diamond slam was cold," he muttered to himself. "Except de way white-Bwana playin' it."

The four finalists were soon assembled in the main grain compound. Some twenty kibitzers were surrounding the table when play began. This board arrived early in the first set:

```
Love all            ♠ 7 3
Dealer South        ♡ 8 3
                    ◇ Q 10 7 5 3
                    ♣ J 8 7 2
  ♠ Q 9 5 4         N          ♠ 10 8 6 2
  ♡ K J 7 5 2    W     E       ♡ Q 9 6
  ◇ K 2             S          ◇ 9 8 6
  ♣ 6 5                        ♣ 10 9 3
                    ♠ A K J
                    ♡ A 10 4
                    ◇ A J 4
                    ♣ A K Q 4
```

South	West	North	East
The	Miss	Bro.	Mrs.
Parrot	Nabooba	Tobias	Okoku
2 ♣	No	2 ◇	No
3NT	End		

Miss Nabooba, wearing one of her favourite low-cut dresses in lime green, led ♡ 5 against 3NT. Mrs. Okoku won with the queen and returned the 9. The Parrot paused for thought. What should he do? One line was to hold up the heart ace until the third round and then cash the ace of diamonds, guarding against a singleton king with West. If East had the king of diamonds she was welcome to win a trick with it. She would have no heart to return unless the suit was breaking 4-4.

Suddenly a better plan occurred to him. Yes, throw West in with the third round of hearts. What would happen then? Assuming West had a five-card heart suit, declarer would have to find two discards when the hearts were run. That meant he could afford to cash only two clubs before the throw-in. Otherwise West's last heart would embarrass him.

"The ace of hearts, he ate some tarts," declared the Parrot, extracting the heart ace from his card holder and tossing it onto the table. *"All on a summer's day."*

"Leave out de cabaret," snapped Mrs. Okoku. "Six rubbers takin' long time an' it gettin' powerful hot in hour or two."

The Parrot cashed the ace-king of clubs and exited with ♡ 10. Miss Nabooba won with the jack and cashed a fourth round of hearts, the Parrot discarding a low diamond. These cards remained:

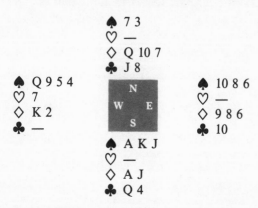

```
                    ♠ 7 3
                    ♡ —
                    ◇ Q 10 7
                    ♣ J 8
   ♠ Q 9 5 4                      ♠ 10 8 6
   ♡ 7          N                 ♡ —
   ◇ K 2      W   E               ◇ 9 8 6
   ♣ —            S               ♣ 10
                    ♠ A K J
                    ♡ —
                    ◇ A J
                    ♣ Q 4
```

On West's last heart the Parrot discarded the queen of clubs. Miss Nabooba now studied her hand resignedly. Obviously she did not hold the outstanding club.

"After taking three rounds of hearts," chanted the Parrot, *"Poor West was left on play."*

Dr. Rutter and several of the kibitzers chuckled at this, but Miss

Nabooba was not amused. "Let me know when you's finished makin' a fool of yourself," she said. "Then I's gonna leadin' de 4 of spades."

The prospect of a spade switch into his tenace managed to silence the Parrot. He won with the jack and claimed nine tricks.

"Six clubs is pretty good, isn't it?" said Brother Tobias, trying to distract attention from his partner's excellent play. "Needs a heart lead to crack it, I think."

A couple of hands later the two women levelled the scores with a straightforward game in no-trumps. Then this hand arrived:

Game all
Dealer West

♠ K
♡ A Q 9 4
◇ A K 8
♣ A K Q 9 2

♠ A 5
♡ K 10 8 7 3
◇ 9 7 3 2
♣ 6 5

♠ Q J 10 9 7 6 2
♡ —
◇ J 5
♣ J 10 8 3

♠ 8 4 3
♡ J 6 5 2
◇ Q 10 6 4
♣ 7 4

South	West	North	East
The	Miss	Bro.	Mrs.
Parrot	Nabooba	Tobias	Okoku
—	No	2♣	2♠
No	No	Dble	No
3♡	No	4♡	End

Miss Nabooba eyed her glittering line of trumps contentedly, looking forward to the moment when the Parrot would discover the bad break. She led the ace of spades and continued with another spade to weaken the dummy's trump holding. The Parrot ruffed with the 4 and led the queen of hearts from dummy, East discarding a small spade.

"No hearts, partner?" asked Miss Nabooba, with a sideways glance at the Parrot.

Mrs. Okoku thumbed through her cards, shaking her head. "I ain't got none," she replied. "Parrot-bird must havin' 'em all."

Miss Nabooba won the trick with the king of hearts. Unfortunately for her, she had no further spade to return. She switched to a diamond, won in hand by declarer.

The Parrot perked up at this reprieve; perhaps the contract could be made after all. He finessed the 9 of trumps and cashed the ace. He then unblocked dummy's diamond honours and started on the clubs. On the third round he discarded his remaining spade loser from hand. Miss Nabooba ruffed the trick but was helpless. Her last two cards were ♡ 10 and ◇ 9. The Parrot held ♡ J and ◇ 10.

There was an enthusiastic round of applause from the kibitzers and the Parrot hopped round on his perch to give a little bow.

Dr. Rutter, the visiting ornithologist, had been watching the Parrot's performance with increasing amazement. "*Rara avis in terris nigroque simillimo cygno*," he exclaimed, recalling the poet Juvenal.

"What did you say?" said the Parrot, spinning round.

"Words of admiration, I assure you," declared Dr. Rutter. "It was Latin, actually."

"I know that!" squawked the Parrot. "It should be *simillima*, not *simillimo*; feminine to agree with *avis*. It's a hexameter, meaning 'a rare bird on this earth, like a black swan'."

Dr. Rutter extracted a massive tome from an inside pocket and adjusted his pince-nez. "I must make a note of this for my next lecture at the Royal Society," he said.

"I don't know a lot of Latin," said the Parrot modestly.

"Shall we proceed with our game?" interrupted Brother Tobias. "We don't want any swelled heads, do we?"

The two women fought back strongly to take the next rubber. They were leading by about 300 aggregate points when this hand arrived, early in the third rubber.

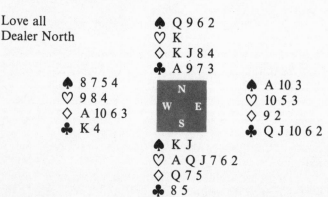

Love all
Dealer North

♠ Q 9 6 2
♡ K
◇ K J 8 4
♣ A 9 7 3

♠ 8 7 5 4
♡ 9 8 4
◇ A 10 6 3
♣ K 4

♠ A 10 3
♡ 10 5 3
◇ 9 2
♣ Q J 10 6 2

♠ K J
♡ A Q J 7 6 2
◇ Q 7 5
♣ 8 5

South	West	North	East
The	Miss	Bro.	Mrs.
Parrot	Nabooba	Tobias	Okoku
—	—	1◇	No
1♡	No	1♠	No
4♡	End		

The Parrot, who always hogged the bidding when playing with Brother Tobias, raised himself to four hearts at his second turn. Clubs were the unbid suit and Miss Nabooba opted for the bold lead of the club king. The Parrot won in dummy, unblocked the king of trumps and attempted to reach his hand by leading a spade. Mrs. Okoku leapt in with the ace and made the cunning return of ♣ 10, hoping that the Parrot would assume the opening lead had been from a K–Q–J sequence.

The club ten held the trick and Mrs. Okoku maintained the illusion by continuing with ♣ 6. The Parrot ruffed with a low trump and stretched out a claw to gather the trick.

"Dis trick's mine, I think," said Miss Nabooba, overruffing.

The Parrot's beak fell open in disbelief. Miss Nabooba cashed the ace of diamonds and the game was one down.

"You sure polishin' de mirror on dat one, Doris," chuckled Miss Nabooba. "Nice card, dat ten of clubs."

Mr. Ghu, an elderly kibitzer in the front row, leaned forward to address the Parrot. "Couldn't you makin' dat one?" he enquired. "Safer to ruffin' de club high, isn't it?"

"Of course not!" squawked the Parrot. "Then you'd need trumps 3–3."

"Yes, but they were," confirmed Mr. Ghu. "Miss Nabooba havin' three and Mrs. Okoku havin' three. Dey both havin' three trumps. If you makin' de safety play of ruffin' high, ten tricks are easily there."

The Parrot, not one to suffer fools gladly, looked across the table, hoping to enlist some support from his partner.

"I think this gentleman has a good point," observed Brother Tobias.

An hour or so later the final was nearing its conclusion. In spite of the shade provided by the cola trees that surrounded the grain compound, the contestants were already suffering from the heat of the late morning.

"Phew! Sun-god workin' overtime today," exclaimed Mrs. Okoku, fanning herself furiously. Her fan, made of red-dyed chicken feathers, had been a silver wedding present from the late Mr. Okoku.

Brother Tobias glared at her. "As I've tried to make clear a hundred times, Doris," he said, "the sun is a mere mass of burning gas. It has no connection with any deity whatsoever."

There was a sudden intake of breath from the kibitzers present. "Ssh, Bwana!" said Miss Nabooba, looking round nervously. "If Sun-god hear you don't believin' in him, he mos' probably burnin' de village down."

"I sometimes think that Brother Luke and myself are wasting our time here," said Brother Tobias, wiping his forehead with a large white handkerchief. "Your call, I think."

Love all
Dealer North

♠ J 8 3
♡ A 8 6
◇ A
♣ A Q J 9 8 7

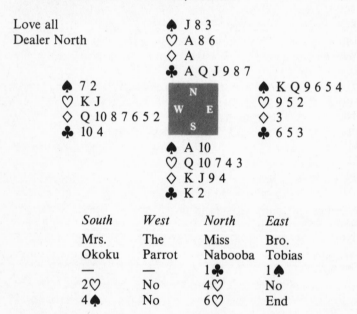

♠ 7 2
♡ K J
◇ Q 10 8 7 6 5 2
♣ 10 4

♠ K Q 9 6 5 4
♡ 9 5 2
◇ 3
♣ 6 5 3

♠ A 10
♡ Q 10 7 4 3
◇ K J 9 4
♣ K 2

South	West	North	East
Mrs.	The	Miss	Bro.
Okoku	Parrot	Nabooba	Tobias
—	—	1♣	1♠
2♡	No	4♡	No
4♠	No	6♡	End

A crisp auction from the ladies left Mrs. Okoku in six hearts. The Parrot led ♠ 7 and East's queen forced the ace. Prospects were poor. The only chance was to start by discarding the spade loser on dummy's clubs. Presumably one of the defenders would ruff the third round of clubs. Declarer would then have to pick up the remaining trumps without loss.

Mrs. Okoku cashed two rounds of clubs successfully. On the third round she discarded her spade loser and the Parrot ruffed deceptively with the king. Back came another spade but Mrs. Okoku had a triumphant glint in her eye. Surely she could pick up East's J–9–5–2 in trumps by playing good clubs through him! She ruffed the spade

exit, crossed to the diamond ace and led another club. She smiled
confidently at her partner. If East ruffed with one of his four trumps,
she would overruff and cross to the heart ace to lead yet another high
club. If, instead, East let all the clubs pass, she would lead ♡ 8 from
dummy, forcing a cover with the 9. She could then return to the ace of
trumps to finesse against East's jack. Yes, the contract was cold.

East and South both discarded on the fourth round of clubs, and
Mrs. Okoku's smile vanished in an instant when the Parrot ruffed the
trick with the jack of trumps. When a diamond was returned, Mrs.
Okoku avoided the indignity of a second undertrick by ruffing with
the ace and subsequently running the 8 of trumps. This play was
marked because the Parrot would obviously not have risked
a false card from ♡ K J x. The contract was therefore one down.

"What happened there?" queried a mystified Brother Tobias. "Did
you mean to ruff that first club with the king?"

"Pulled the wrong card! Pulled the wrong card!" squawked the
Parrot, winking at the nearest kibitzer.

Brother Tobias shook his head at this piece of carelessness and
began to deal the next hand.

With a flutter of feathers the Parrot jumped on the table. "Of
COURSE I meant to ruff with the king!" he screeched. "She makes it
easily if I ruff with the jack."

"All right, all right," said Brother Tobias. "There's no need to
over-react. You don't see me jumping on the table every time
I make a clever play, do you?"

"No," replied the Parrot, resuming his perch. "Fortunately for the
table."

The penultimate rubber had reached Game All when this hand was
dealt:

Game all

Dealer South

♠ Q 6 3
♡ K 7 5
◇ Q 8
♣ K J 10 6 2

♠ 10 7 4
♡ 8 4 2
◇ J 7 6 4 3
♣ 5 3

♠ A K J 2
♡ J 10 6 3
◇ 10 9 5
♣ Q 8

♠ 9 8 5
♡ A Q 9
◇ A K 2
♣ A 9 7 4

South	*West*	*North*	*East*
Mrs.	The	Miss	Bro.
Okoku	Parrot	Nabooba	Tobias
1NT	No	3NT	End

The Parrot's hand was so weak that he saw little future in attacking in diamonds. Hoping to hit his partner's suit, he led ♠ 4. Brother Tobias won with the jack and cashed the spade ace. Then, trying to create the illusion that he had no more spades left, he switched to ◇ 10.

Mrs. Okoku won in dummy and crossed to the ace of clubs, noting East's 8 with interest. Could that be a singleton? Anyhow, she needed only four tricks from the suit; she must obviously finesse clubs into the safe hand to make sure of the contract.

Brother Tobias won with the club queen and, after a short pause for dramatic effect, cashed two more rounds of spades to beat the contract. "You see?" he said to the Parrot. "Here I am, still in my chair. I haven't jumped on the table, have I?"

"Couldn't you readin' dat one, Doris?" said Miss Nabooba, concerned at the number of opportunities they had let slip. "If Parrot-bird havin' five spades, he mos' probably playin' de 2 on second round."

"Not necessarily," replied Mrs. Okoku loftily. "Some people playin' dat de second card is suit preference. Anyhow, I ain't goin' to give up doin' safety plays jus' because one of 'em don' workin'."

On the next hand Brother Tobias won the rubber for his side with a somewhat fortunate heart game. The ladies entered the final rubber 1250 points adrift. They were already one game ahead when Mrs. Okoku picked up this collection:

♠ A K 7
♡ A J
◇ A K Q J 10
♣ A K 5

She gazed gratefully at the dazzling array of honour cards. Hah!
The Sun-god had rewarded her for believing in him. Sun-god be
praised! Surely there would be a slam somewhere and they would win
the cup. "Two clubs," she said, giving her partner the good news.

The two diamond response came as no surprise. Mrs. Okoku
pressed on with three diamonds and Miss Nabooba bid three hearts.
Mrs. Okoku consulted her scoresheet. Would it be enough to win the
match if she made 3NT? 700 for rubber . . . 130 for ten tricks . . . and
150 for honours. No, they would still lose by over a hundred. It had
to be a slam. Surely the Sun-god wouldn't give her a Yarborough in
the dummy. "Six no-trumps," she said.

This was the full deal:

North–South game
Dealer South

♠ 8 6 4
♡ K 9 6 3
◇ 7 5
♣ 8 7 4 2

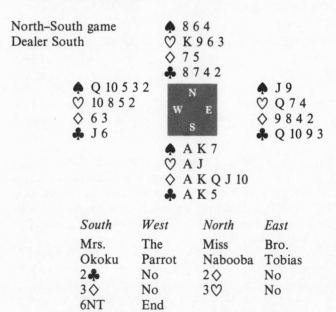

♠ Q 10 5 3 2   ♠ J 9
♡ 10 8 5 2   ♡ Q 7 4
◇ 6 3   ◇ 9 8 4 2
♣ J 6   ♣ Q 10 9 3

♠ A K 7
♡ A J
◇ A K Q J 10
♣ A K 5

South	West	North	East
Mrs.	The	Miss	Bro.
Okoku	Parrot	Nabooba	Tobias
2♣	No	2◇	No
3◇	No	3♡	No
6NT	End		

It was by no means obvious what the Parrot should lead. A black-
suit lead seemed out of the question – much too dangerous. A diamond

lead was a possibility but it might damage an honour in partner's hand. Eventually the Parrot led ♡ 2 and Mrs. Okoku played the 9 from dummy, hoping to tempt East into an indiscretion. Brother Tobias, not giving the matter much thought, covered with the queen and the trick was won with the ace.

Mrs. Okoku observed that the contract could easily be made if clubs were 3–3. Still, the first move must be to run the diamonds. The Parrot, sitting West, threw a heart, a spade and a club on the diamonds. When the ace–king of clubs followed, this was the end position:

Miss Nabooba
♠ 8
♡ K 6
◇ —
♣ 8 7 4

The Parrot
♠ Q 10 5 3
♡ 10 8
◇ —
♣ —

Bro. Tobias
♠ J
♡ 7 4
◇ —
♣ Q 10 9

♠ A K 7
♡ J
◇ —
♣ K 5
Mrs. Okoku

The Parrot was reluctant to throw another spade on the king of clubs. If he did, declarer might cash two spades and the jack of hearts and endplay him in spades to give dummy the last trick with the king of hearts. The Parrot therefore discarded a heart. Mrs. Okoku clucked at this stroke of misfortune. Her main chance had gone; the clubs were not breaking.

When the ace–king of spades followed, Brother Tobias found he was in the same position as the Parrot had been. To prevent Mrs. Okoku overtaking the jack of hearts and scoring two heart tricks, he had to bare the club queen and retain two hearts. Mrs. Okoku cashed the jack of hearts and stared at her last two cards, a low spade and a low club. Which should she play? Surely the Parrot had two spades left. Yes, a club it had to be. Brother Tobias won with the queen of clubs and, somewhat reluctantly, faced his last card — a heart to dummy's king.

"Dat was real swish performance, Doris!" exclaimed Miss Nabooba. "A mos' beautiful throw-in play."

"Well, de hand jus' playin' itself really," replied Mrs. Okoku, unsure exactly what had happened.

"It wouldn't have played itself if the queen of hearts had been held up at trick one," observed the Parrot, hopping up and down in irritated fashion.

Brother Tobias rose to his feet, muttered a few words of congratulation to the victors, then walked disconsolately from the table.

With a flurry of feathers the Parrot took off and alighted on Brother Tobias's shoulder. "I still think our God's better than their Sun-God," he squawked. "It's just that six rubbers isn't really long enough for the difference to show."

11

The Witchdoctor's Prize Mixture

The twice-weekly rubber bridge sessions at the Bozwambi settlement were played for modest stakes – 10 mpengos (about 2p) a hundred. For some while there had been talk among the better players of forming a high stake game.

Mbozi poked his head into the Witchdoctor's hut. "You playin' in de rubber game tonight?" he enquired.

The Witchdoctor, who was mixing some powders in an old copper kettle, shook his head. "For 10 mpengos?" he said. "Waste of time. Anyhow, we's not welcome in dat game. De bad players jus' thinkin' we's load of vultures, swoopin' on 'em."

"We could fixin' nice private game at 100 mpengos," suggested Mbozi. "Mebbe Mrs. Okoku and Miss Nabooba like to playin'. You think they havin' enough money?"

"Okoku woman well loaded," replied the Witchdoctor knowledgeably. "An' if Miss Nabooba runnin' out of money . . . hah!" he bared his yellow teeth in an evil grin, "dere's plenty other ways she can settlin' up with us."

"Dat's OK if we's winnin'," agreed Mbozi. "But what if dey's hittin' a good streak and we can't payin' up. Mebbe Mrs. Okoku callin' us to her hut in middle of de night."

The Witchdoctor gave a hideous sniff and reached for his copper kettle once more. "Can't riskin' dat possibility," he declared. "Better askin' Parrot-bird and Mjubu. If we startin' at 6 o'clock we got plenty of time to takin' 'em to de cleaners."

At the appointed hour the four players met in the Witchdoctor's hut. All sat cross-legged on the floor except the Parrot, who preferred to play standing up. Two dull part-scores were followed by this deal:

Love all   ♠ K 10 8 2
Dealer East   ♡ K 8 3
       ◇ A Q 6
       ♣ 5 4 2

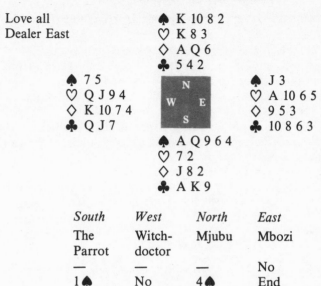

♠ 7 5   ♠ J 3
♡ Q J 9 4   ♡ A 10 6 5
◇ K 10 7 4   ◇ 9 5 3
♣ Q J 7   ♣ 10 8 6 3

       ♠ A Q 9 6 4
       ♡ 7 2
       ◇ J 8 2
       ♣ A K 9

South	*West*	*North*	*East*
The	Witch-	Mjubu	Mbozi
Parrot	doctor		
—	—	—	No
1♠	No	4♠	End

The Witchdoctor led the queen of hearts against four spades and the Parrot played low from the dummy. Hearts were continued and the Parrot ruffed the third round.

There was a certain club loser, so declarer would have to find the diamond king onside and then achieve some sort of elimination ending. The Parrot drew trumps in two rounds, then played a club to the king. The Witchdoctor, who as usual was well up with the play, unblocked the queen from the West seat. The Parrot continued with the ace of clubs and the Witchdoctor stopped to think. Should he unblock the jack now? That would look silly if the Parrot had the 10 of clubs and East held the jack of diamonds. Still, thought the Witchdoctor, with ♣ A K 10 the Parrot would probably have taken a deep finesse in the suit. Yes, the jack of clubs must be the right card.

The Parrot finessed the diamond queen successfully, then exited in clubs. Thanks to the double unblock by the Witchdoctor, Mbozi was able to win the third round of clubs in the East seat. A diamond from his side of the table gave nothing away, so the contract went one down.

"Hah! Dat was nifty piece of defendin'," exclaimed the Witchdoctor, cracking his finger joints. "Now, you gennulmen like to joinin' me for special treat?"

"One of your cocktails, you meanin'?" said Mbozi dubiously. "De Cannibal's Relish with de gunpowder in it?"

"Dat's all finished long ago," replied the Witchdoctor. "Mos' unfortunate but one of de ingredients I can only gettin' from Zbolwumba tribe. Dey ain't been callin' recently."

The Witchdoctor opened one of his medicine chests and produced a long clay pipe, which he proceeded to fill with the mixture of powders from the copper kettle. "Dis powerful good smoke," he declared, lighting the pipe with an old-fashioned tinder. "We can passin' de pipe round as we play."

The next hand was soon dealt.

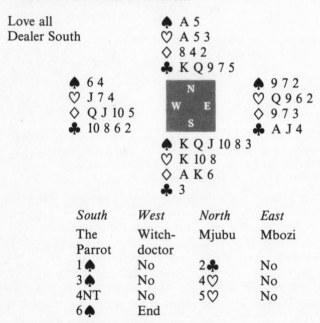

Love all
Dealer South

♠ A 5
♡ A 5 3
◇ 8 4 2
♣ K Q 9 7 5

♠ 6 4
♡ J 7 4
◇ Q J 10 5
♣ 10 8 6 2

♠ 9 7 2
♡ Q 9 6 2
◇ 9 7 3
♣ A J 4

♠ K Q J 10 8 3
♡ K 10 8
◇ A K 6
♣ 3

South	West	North	East
The Parrot	Witch- doctor	Mjubu	Mbozi
1♠	No	2♣	No
3♠	No	4♡	No
4NT	No	5♡	No
6♠	End		

The Witchdoctor drew deeply on the pipe, rolled his eyes in ecstasy, then led the queen of diamonds. The Parrot won the trick and played a club to the king. The Witchdoctor petered with the 8, showing an even number of clubs, and Mbozi won with the ace.

Declarer was marked with a singleton club, so Mbozi could see there were insufficient entries to establish and run the club suit. Deciding against any heroics in the heart suit, he exited passively in diamonds. The Parrot won in hand and played the king and ace of trumps. He then cashed the queen of clubs, throwing a diamond, and ruffed a club high. When he ran the trump suit, this ending resulted:

Mjubu
♠ —
♡ A 5
♢ 8
♣ 9

Witchdoctor
♠ —
♡ J 7
♢ J
♣ 10

Mbozi
♠ —
♡ Q 9 6
♢ 9
♣ —

♠ 8
♡ K 10 8
♢ —
♣ —

The Parrot

On the last trump the Witchdoctor obviously could not afford a club. And if he threw a heart, declarer would be able to pick up the heart suit with the aid of a second-round finesse against East's queen.

Eventually the Witchdoctor decided to throw the jack of diamonds. Dummy's club was thrown and Mbozi found he was squeezed in the red suits. He discarded a heart and the Parrot scored three heart tricks to make the contract.

The Witchdoctor blinked. "You dozin' off, Mbozi?" he cried. "What's dis pathetic diamond return when you winnin' de club ace? You should switchin' to a heart."

Mbozi, whose turn it was with the pipe, puffed away in silence. A heart return? Would that have made any difference?

The Parrot looked distastefully at the cloud of strangely-scented smoke, flapping it away with his wing. "No good! No good!" he exclaimed. "Eight forces the jack, then I can finesse. Same if you play the nine, I cover with the ten."

The Witchdoctor glowered at the Parrot. "Course he don' playin' *low* heart," he said. "He playin' de queen. Now you's finished."

The Parrot had an idea there was an answer to this, but a sudden intake of infected air caused him to break into a violent cough.

"You like to tryin' a smoke?" said Mbozi, offering the pipe to the Parrot. "Smokin' make de cough better right away."

The Parrot looked at the pipe suspiciously. "That's hashish, isn't it?" he said.

The Witchdoctor laughed. "Hashish only de start of it," he said. "Also ginja root, crushed beetle wings and droppings of jungle chicken."

The Parrot put the pipe in his beak and drew a deep breath, causing the mixture in the bowl to crackle loudly. The other players leaned forward, awaiting his verdict with interest.

The Parrot took the pipe from his beak, blew out a great cloud of smoke and turned towards the Witchdoctor. "Quite an impertinent little blend," he informed him. "Somewhat light on the beetles' wings, perhaps."

12

Chief Bazoogah's Revenge

The Parrot's improvement at the game had been so evident that it was no longer possible to exclude him from the Bozwambi league team. His debut was to be against the middle-of-the-table Mazemmutot Pygmies. This was an away fixture, requiring a full day's trek by elephant. When the team arrived at the Mazemmutot settlement, they were exhausted.

"Ah . . . welcome, welcome!" said the diminutive Chief Bazoogah, pleased to see his opponents looking so weary. "You findin' us all right, then?"

"Yes, no thanks to the route suggested on your map," replied Brother Tobias, dismounting from the howdah. "We found ourselves in the middle of a swamp at one stage. The elephant was up to its haunches in the most foul-smelling mud."

"Ah, dat mus' be Mpistole swamp," replied the Chieftain. "Quite passable at dis time of year." The Chieftain gazed curiously at the Parrot who had just fluttered onto Brother Tobias's shoulder. "What's dat?" he enquired. "De team mascot?"

"Er . . . no," replied Brother Tobias. "He's a member of our team. A fully-fledged member, one might say."

"He play in de team?" cackled the Chieftain. "De elephant playin' too?"

Battle commenced with this deal:

North–South game
Dealer North

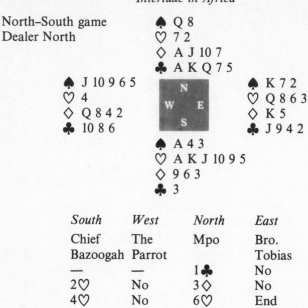

```
            ♠ Q 8
            ♡ 7 2
            ◇ A J 10 7
            ♣ A K Q 7 5
♠ J 10 9 6 5              ♠ K 7 2
♡ 4                      ♡ Q 8 6 3
◇ Q 8 4 2                ◇ K 5
♣ 10 8 6                 ♣ J 9 4 2
            ♠ A 4 3
            ♡ A K J 10 9 5
            ◇ 9 6 3
            ♣ 3
```

South	West	North	East
Chief	The	Mpo	Bro.
Bazoogah	Parrot		Tobias
—	—	1♣	No
2♡	No	3◇	No
4♡	No	6♡	End

The Parrot led the jack of spades and cast a beady eye over the North player when the dummy appeared. Jumping straight to six with no spade control? These opponents would obviously need watching.

The spade jack was covered by the queen, king and ace. Chief Bazoogah then cashed three rounds of clubs to dispose of his spade losers. A finesse of the trump jack succeeded and declarer turned his attention to diamonds, hoping to re-enter dummy eventually for a second trump finesse. After a low diamond to the jack and king, Brother Tobias returned the jack of clubs. The Chieftain ruffed with the 9 and the Parrot calmly discarded the queen of diamonds.

Chief Bazoogah, who was sitting on two thick cushions to prevent his hand being overlooked, inspected this card carefully. Eventually he decided it was too dangerous to play another diamond. He cashed the ace of trumps from hand, hoping the suit would divide 3–2.

When the Parrot showed out on this trick, the Chieftain had to make a last-ditch attempt at a trump reduction. He crossed to the ace of diamonds and ruffed dummy's last spade. With ♡ K J and ◇ 9 remaining, he needed to reach dummy just one more time. Whispering a silent prayer, he led ◇ 9 and overtook with dummy's 10. His prayers never reached their destination. Brother Tobias ruffed the trick and the slam was one down.

"What happened there?" said Brother Tobias, giving his partner a puzzled glance. "How many diamonds did you start with?"

"Queen doubleton," squawked the Parrot, chortling to himself, ". . . and a couple of small ones."

Meanwhile the Witchdoctor and Mbozi were piling on the points against the Chieftain's two sons, each as pint-sized as the other.

Game all
Dealer South

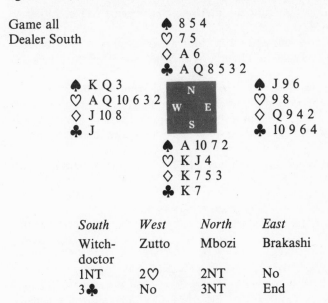

```
              ♠ 8 5 4
              ♡ 7 5
              ◇ A 6
              ♣ A Q 8 5 3 2
♠ K Q 3                        ♠ J 9 6
♡ A Q 10 6 3 2    N            ♡ 9 8
◇ J 10 8       W     E         ◇ Q 9 4 2
♣ J              S             ♣ 10 9 6 4
              ♠ A 10 7 2
              ♡ K J 4
              ◇ K 7 5 3
              ♣ K 7
```

South	West	North	East
Witch-doctor	Zutto	Mbozi	Brakashi
1NT	2♡	2NT	No
3♣	No	3NT	End

Mbozi's 2NT call was Lebensohl – a transfer to three clubs. When followed by 3NT it denied four spades and showed a desire to play in the no-trump game if partner had a heart stop. A direct call of 3NT would have promised a heart stop in his own hand.

Against the no-trump game West led a heart to the 8 and jack. The Witchdoctor would have liked to open the club suit by leading towards his king-seven, hoping to duck the trick to West – the safe hand. Unfortunately he could not spare the diamond ace as an entry. Spotting a small extra chance, he decided to lead ♣ 7 from hand. When by good fortune the jack appeared on his left, he ducked the trick. West switched to a diamond, but the Witchdoctor won in hand, unblocked the club king and crossed in diamonds to run the club suit. Nine tricks were made for +600.

In the other room the Parrot was sitting West. This was the auction:

South	West	North	East
Chief	The	Mpo	Bro.
Bazoogah	Parrot		Tobias
1NT	2♡	3♣	No
3NT	End		

Unwilling to lead into declarer's presumed heart tenace, the Parrot tried his luck with the jack of diamonds. Declarer won with the king and played the king and ace of clubs. He then led a low club to East's 10, establishing the suit. Brother Tobias returned ♡ 9 to the jack and queen, and the Parrot exited with ◊ 10.

The Chieftain now ran the club suit, hoping that West would be inconvenienced in the end position. It was not to be. The Parrot retained a low diamond, killing any possibility of a throw in. The contract eventually went one down and the Bozwambi team scored a healthy swing.

The last hand before the tea interval found the Witchdoctor in a delicate slam.

Love all
Dealer North

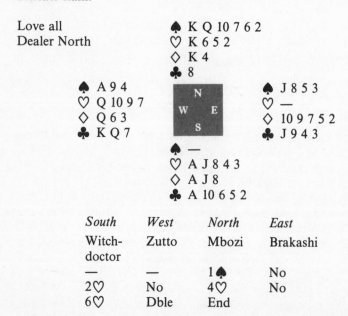

	♠ K Q 10 7 6 2	
	♡ K 6 5 2	
	◊ K 4	
	♣ 8	
♠ A 9 4		♠ J 8 5 3
♡ Q 10 9 7		♡ —
◊ Q 6 3		◊ 10 9 7 5 2
♣ K Q 7		♣ J 9 4 3
	♠ —	
	♡ A J 8 4 3	
	◊ A J 8	
	♣ A 10 6 5 2	

South	West	North	East
Witch-	Zutto	Mbozi	Brakashi
doctor			
—	—	1♠	No
2♡	No	4♡	No
6♡	Dble	End	

Two hands previously the Witchdoctor had gone three off undoubled in an absurd spade game. Zutto had spoken sharply to his partner for not doubling the contract. On this occasion there was therefore no question of allowing six hearts to go unpunished. Zutto doubled and spun the king of clubs onto the wicker card table.

It seemed to the Witchdoctor that a crossruff offered reasonable prospects. He won the club lead, ruffed a club and led the king of spades. When East followed impassively with a low card, the Witchdoctor ruffed the trick in hand. After cashing the two top diamonds, he took four further ruffs to arrive at this ending:

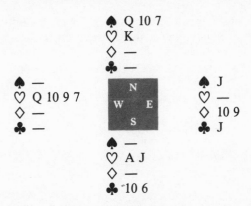

```
              ♠ Q 10 7
              ♡ K
              ◇ —
              ♣ —
♠ —                          ♠ J
♡ Q 10 9 7      N            ♡ —
◇ —         W       E        ◇ 10 9
♣ —             S            ♣ J
              ♠ —
              ♡ A J
              ◇ —
              ♣ 10 6
```

With a triumphant leer at his left-hand opponent the Witchdoctor ruffed a club with the king and exited with the queen of spades. West had to ruff the trick and lead into the Witchdoctor's trump tenace, giving him twelve tricks.

"What's dis double?" demanded Brakashi, jumping off his pile of cushions and peering over the edge of the card table at his partner. "You handin' him de distribution on a plate, jus' to try and gettin' extra 50?"

"Extra 50? I's expectin' at least 500," protested his partner, retrieving his cards from the table. "Look! King-queen of clubs, de spade bullet, de diamond queen, four trumps to queen-ten! Only blidderin' idiot wouldn't double on dat collection!"

At half-time the Bozwambi team led by the satisfactory margin of 27 IMPs.

"Can you makin' dat slam on trump lead?" enquired Mbozi as the players walked towards the Chieftain's hut where the tea was to be served. "You havin' too much work to do, isn't it?"

"You's right, I think," replied the Witchdoctor, with a chuckle. "Hah! Dat would be some lead to find."

The competitors seated themselves round a large table and the main course was served, jungle-chicken couscous.

"Good gracious, these are small servings," muttered Brother Tobias, prodding his portion with a fork. "You'd have thought they would have made some allowance for us being much bigger than they are."

"Speak for yourself," retorted the Parrot, bending forward to help himself to a beakful. "Mind you, I've never been that keen on jungle-chicken." He pushed his plate to one side. "Makes me feel like a cannibal."

A Pygmy waiter stepped forward to remove the Parrot's plate but Brother Tobias just beat him to it. "Waste not what the good Lord hath provided," he declared.

When the match restarted Chief Bazoogah was soon in action.

Game all   ♠ Q 10 7 2
Dealer East   ♡ K 10 3
                ◇ 10 8 4
                ♣ J 3 2

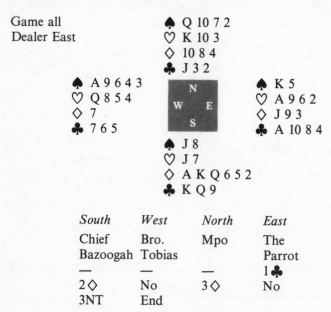

♠ A 9 6 4 3	♠ K 5
♡ Q 8 5 4	♡ A 9 6 2
◇ 7	◇ J 9 3
♣ 7 6 5	♣ A 10 8 4

                ♠ J 8
                ♡ J 7
                ◇ A K Q 6 5 2
                ♣ K Q 9

South	West	North	East
Chief	Bro.	Mpo	The
Bazoogah	Tobias		Parrot
—	—	—	1♣
2◇	No	3◇	No
3NT	End		

The Pygmy chieftain, obviously impressed by his two half-stops in the majors, decided to try his luck in 3NT. Brother Tobias led ♠ 4 and the Parrot won with the king. There was no future in the spade suit so the Parrot switched to ♡ 2. Declarer played the 7 and Brother Tobias's queen forced the dummy's king. It was now a simple matter for declarer to force out the club ace, giving him nine tricks.

"Unbelievable!" screeched the Parrot. "Unbe-flapping-LIEV-ABLE!"

"What are you on about now?" queried Brother Tobias.

"Play the 8, play the 8," squawked the Parrot, hopping up and down in agitated fashion.

"Oh, in hearts, you mean," said Brother Tobias, light dawning. "Yes, that does get it off as the cards lie; I can pin the jack on the next round. It costs a trick if you hold jack-nine to four, of course."

The Parrot stared curiously at Brother Tobias, wondering what process of reasoning could lead to such a stupid remark. "Fat chance of getting it off if I hold jack-nine to four," he remarked.

"Are you determined to make me look small?" demanded Brother Tobias. "Sometimes I think partnership morale is a complete irrelevance to you."

"Look small?" queried the Chieftain fiercely. "What's dis meanin'?"

Brother Tobias gave an embarrassed laugh and prodded his enormous bulk with a forefinger. "Just a private joke," he replied.

A few hands later Brother Tobias spotted a chance to redeem himself. Sitting West at Love All he picked up:

♠ Q 8 6 2
♡ A K Q 10 8 3
♢ A 3
♣ 6

His opening call of one heart was doubled by North. The Parrot raised pre-emptively to three hearts and Chief Bazoogah, sitting South, jumped to five diamonds.

Brother Tobias studied his hand once more. It seemed likely that there would be several spade losers in five hearts. Better to take a chance on beating five diamonds, surely. "No bid," he said.

Five diamonds was passed out and Brother Tobias decided to lead his singleton club, hoping that he might be able to reach his partner's hand when in with the trump ace. The elderly North player leaned forward to display the dummy:

♠ A K 7 3
♡ 7
◇ Q 10 5
♣ K Q 9 8 2

♠ Q 8 6 2
♡ A K Q 10 8 3
◇ A 3
♣ 6

South	West	North	East
Chief	Bro.	Mpo	The
Bazoogah	Tobias		Parrot
—	1♡	Dble	3♡
5◇	End		

Declarer played low from dummy on the club lead and won East's ten with the ace. When a low trump appeared from declarer's hand, Brother Tobias pounced with the ace, North and East following small. It was clear that the only chance to beat the contract was to cross to partner's hand for a club ruff. Brother Tobias therefore continued with ♡3, a McKenney signal requesting a club return.

When the Parrot played ♡9 and declarer won with the jack, Brother Tobias gave a wry smile. "Sorry, partner," he said. "I could have saved an IMP here."

"Only one?" cackled Chief Bazoogah, leading another round of trumps from hand. "I mus' makin' de remainin' tricks now. Except for de king of trumps, of course."

This had been the full hand:

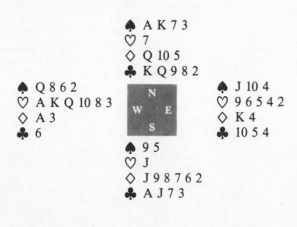

♠ A K 7 3
♡ 7
◇ Q 10 5
♣ K Q 9 8 2

♠ Q 8 6 2
♡ A K Q 10 8 3
◇ A 3
♣ 6

♠ J 10 4
♡ 9 6 5 4 2
◇ K 4
♣ 10 5 4

♠ 9 5
♡ J
◇ J 9 8 7 6 2
♣ A J 7 3

The Parrot, ominously silent, glared across the table.

"Spare us another outburst," said Brother Tobias. "You'd have defended in just the same way."

The Parrot raised his eyes to the heavens. Surely his three heart call had marked him with at least one good card? What else could it be but the king of diamonds? With five-card heart support and a virtual yarborough he would have passed or attempted some psychic manoeuvre. Raising hearts on that type of hand would only help the opponents to judge their fit.

"Your double raise made it a near certainty you held the jack of hearts," persisted Brother Tobias. "Swap the two red honours and it would have been my best effort of the season."

In the next hut the Witchdoctor and Mbozi were facing a new partnership, the Chieftain's wife and her elder sister. The Chieftain had dispatched his two sons to bed, obviously blaming them for the first-half deficit.

Game all
Dealer East

```
              ♠ A K J 7
              ♡ A 10 8 3
              ◇ 9 6 4 2
              ♣ 3
♠ 10 5 4                      ♠ Q 9 6 3
♡ 9 4 2          N            ♡ Q J 7 6
◇ 10 8       W     E          ◇ A K Q 3
♣ 9 8 7 6 2      S            ♣ 4
              ♠ 8 2
              ♡ K 5
              ◇ J 7 5
              ♣ A K Q J 10 5
```

South	West	North	East
Witch-doctor	Mrs. Obotu	Mbozi	Mrs. Bazoogah
—	—	—	1♡
3NT	No	5NT	No
6♣	No	No	Dble
End			

Mrs. Bazoogah opened the bidding with one heart and the Witchdoctor made the obvious overcall of 3NT. Well, it seemed obvious to him at any rate.

West passed and Mbozi thumbed through his cards, uncertain what move to make. His partner's call was obviously based on a running minor. But which minor? If it was diamonds a slam was a near certainty. Even if it was clubs, twelve tricks might be there if they could avoid a diamond lead. Perhaps he should call five clubs? If the Witchdoctor corrected to five diamonds, he could then raise to six. Still, wasn't there a horrible risk that the Witchdoctor might read five clubs as a natural call? Explaining to the Parrot why they had landed in five clubs with a singleton trump opposite K x was not an attractive prospect.

Another possibility was four hearts. That would doubtless persuade the Witchdoctor to name his suit. But it might also deter a heart lead. Eventually Mbozi opted for the tactical call of 5NT. When the Witchdoctor bid six clubs, East doubled and West led ♡ 2 to the 8, jack and king.

Muttering to himself in a strange tongue, the Witchdoctor drew trumps. The fifth round was led to this end position:

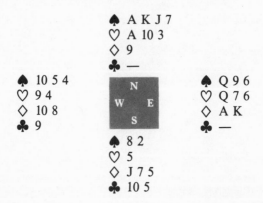

Dummy discarded a spade on ♣ 10 and Mrs. Bazoogah, sitting East, shifted uneasily on her silver-embroidered cushion. A diamond discard would allow the Witchdoctor to establish two diamond tricks if he held three to the jack. A spade discard seemed even more dangerous, so Mrs. Bazoogah decided to throw a heart. The Witchdoctor crossed to the ace of hearts and ruffed a heart, establishing the 10. He then returned to dummy with the spade ace, leaving these cards still in action:

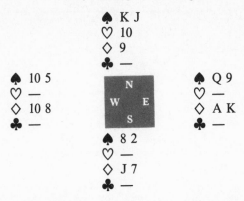

        ♠ K J
        ♡ 10
        ◇ 9
        ♣ —

♠ 10 5   ♠ Q 9
♡ —   ♡ —
◇ 10 8   ◇ A K
♣ —   ♣ —

        ♠ 8 2
        ♡ —
        ◇ J 7
        ♣ —

When ♡ 10 was played Mrs. Bazoogah could scarcely force herself to part with a card. Biting her lip, she threw the ace of diamonds. The Witchdoctor exited with a diamond and dummy's spade tenace claimed the last two tricks.

"You blidderin' dimwit, Olivia!" shouted the Chieftain's wife. "How can you leadin' a heart after I's makin' Lightner Double?"

"Did I mishearin' de biddin'?" replied her partner, much affronted. "You's bidding hearts, isn't it?"

"On diamond lead we gettin' big 800," declared Mrs. Bazoogah, fanning herself furiously. "De double askin' for unusual lead."

Mrs. Obotu scratched her cheek. "I doublin' them for 800 a few hands ago," she said. "You didn't makin' unusual lead then."

Mrs. Bazoogah muttered a swearword under her breath. "Lightner double don' applyin' against 1NT," she said.

A high-scoring final set saw the Bozwambi team home by just 10 IMPs.

"Yes, it was a hard-fought game, as expected," said Brother Tobias, preparing to mount the elephant again. "You can't suggest a better route home, can you? I can't say I'm looking forward to crossing that Mpistole swamp in the dark."

The Pygmy chieftain scribbled a rough map on the back of his scorecard. "Dis mebbe suitin' you better," he said.

The Bozwambi elephant was disappearing into the dusk as Mrs. Bazoogah turned towards her husband. "Dat route you givin' him mus' goin' quite close to Mhadatraz quicksand," she said.

The chieftain put an arm around his wife as they walked back towards their hut. "Quite close?" he chuckled. "Right through de middle of it, you mean."

13

The Witchdoctor's Precaution

The elephant, his front legs half immersed in sand, let out a tremendous bellow of sound.

"Bafaqhassar!" cried the Witchdoctor. "Him sinkin' fast."

Mbozi hauled on the sisal rope that he used to steer the elephant and by some miracle the creature managed to retreat onto firmer ground.

"Do you know what I think?' said Brother Tobias. "That Pygmy chieftain sent us on this route deliberately, just because we beat them."

"Jus' wait till next season when we's de home team," hissed the Witchdoctor. "I's slippin' somethin' powerful nasty into his welcomin' potion."

"Yes, well, make sure the Upper Bhumpopo Bridge Union doesn't hear about it," replied Brother Tobias. "Don't forget the final warning they gave us over that business with the scorpion."

Darkness was approaching, so the team decided to camp out for the night. An oil-lamp provided just enough light for a few rubbers before they went to sleep.

The Witchdoctor's Precaution

Love all
Dealer North

♠ K J 10 7 5 2
♡ K 10
♢ 6
♣ A Q J 8

♠ 9 8 3
♡ Q 5 4
♢ J 9 5 2
♣ K 10 4

♠ A 6 4
♡ J 9 7 6 3 2
♢ A K 8 3
♣ —

♠ Q
♡ A 8
♢ Q 10 7 4
♣ 9 7 6 5 3 2

South	West	North	East
Witch	Bro.	Mbozi	The
doctor	Tobias		Parrot
—	—	1♠	No
2♣	No	4♣	No
4♡	No	5♣	End

The Witchdoctor and Mbozi arrived in five clubs and Brother Tobias led ♢ 2. The Witchdoctor surveyed the dummy approvingly. The game seemed to depend only on the trump finesse – a far better prospect than most of the contracts he played.

The Parrot won the diamond lead deceptively with the ace and returned ♢ 3. When the Witchdoctor made the natural play of the 10, West covered with the jack and dummy ruffed.

The Witchdoctor now returned to hand with the ace of hearts and took a successful trump finesse, East showing out. There was no quick entry to hand to repeat the trump finesse so the Witchdoctor tried the effect of leading dummy's jack of spades.

The Parrot inspected this card with a beady eye, then plunged in with the ace and returned the king of diamonds. Dummy had to ruff with the queen and West's king of trumps could no longer be caught. The game was one down.

"Liked my opening lead, did you?" said Brother Tobias, chortling in the Parrot's direction. "Most people would lead a heart. Just as well I was on lead and not you."

"Certainly was, certainly was," squawked the Parrot. "If you'd been sitting over here, ace and a low diamond would have been quite beyond you."

[97]

Mbozi gave an amused shake of the head at this exchange. If this was the way they congratulated each other after a successful defence, what would happen if a defence misfired?

The first two rubbers were shared and next rubber had reached Game All when this hand was dealt:

Game all
Dealer South

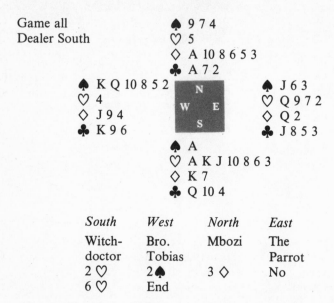

♠ 9 7 4
♥ 5
♦ A 10 8 6 5 3
♣ A 7 2

♠ K Q 10 8 5 2
♥ 4
♦ J 9 4
♣ K 9 6

♠ J 6 3
♥ Q 9 7 2
♦ Q 2
♣ J 8 5 3

♠ A
♥ A K J 10 8 6 3
♦ K 7
♣ Q 10 4

South	West	North	East
Witch-	Bro.	Mbozi	The
doctor	Tobias		Parrot
2 ♥	2 ♠	3 ♦	No
6 ♥	End		

The Witchdoctor never liked to waste time at the bridge table, particularly in the bidding. Brother Tobias led the king of spades against six hearts and the Witchdoctor won with the ace. If both red suits broke 3–2, the contract would be easy. He could play two rounds of trumps, ruff the diamonds good and then concede the master trump. The Witchdoctor therefore started his campaign by banging down the top two trump honours. When West showed out on the second round, the Witchdoctor exited with the ♥ J to East's queen.

The Parrot tilted his head to one side, a valuable aid to concentration. Surely declarer wouldn't have played it this way if he had a spade loser remaining. It seemed the only worthwhile defence must be to attack dummy's club ace, the entry to the diamonds.

When the Parrot returned a low club it was the Witchdoctor's turn to think. His bloodshot eyes flickered backwards and forwards between his own hand and the dummy. The only chance of conserving dummy's club entry was to rise with the queen, playing the Parrot for the king.

The Witchdoctor took a deep breath of the night air as he paused to check his calculations. The Parrot had a great liking for spectacular defensive plays. Surely if the conceited twerp held the king of clubs he would have played it, trying for a Merrimac Coup.

The Witchdoctor pushed the queen of clubs back into his hand and played the 10, covered by the king and ace. He then returned to hand with a spade ruff and ran the trump suit. Brother Tobias had no choice but to keep his three diamonds, so he had to abandon one of the black suits. He decided to keep the spade guard and this ending was reached:

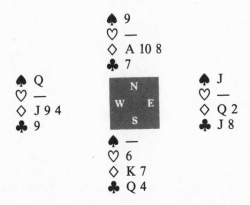

On the last heart West and North both discarded a club. The Parrot scanned his remaining cards, uncertain which one he could spare. Eventually he parted with the jack of spades. The Witchdoctor then cashed the queen of clubs to squeeze West in spades and diamonds. The slam was home.

"Yes, rather a lucky one," observed Brother Tobias. "That puts you . . . let me see, 850 mpengos up, I make it." He rose to his feet. "Shall we settle up in the morning? It's very late."

"Pay NOW!" demanded the Witchdoctor. "We dangerous close to Banzula tribe here. You mebbe gettin' slit up in de night and losin' all de money."

14

The Wildcat Club at Zengali

"You fancy nice trip to de Wildcat Club dis evenin'?" said the Witchdoctor, entering Mbozi's hut one sunny morning.

"Wildcat Club?" replied Mbozi. "What's dat?"

"Hah! You don' hearin' of it?" exclaimed the Witchdoctor. "Dat's de new brothel-hut in Zengali Village."

Mbozi gave a dubious shrug of the shoulders. "How much dat costin' us?" he enquired. "I ain't too flush at de moment."

"Don' costin' single mpengo if we's lucky," replied the Witchdoctor. "De girls all playin' bridge for de house. If you losin' a rubber you payin' 'em de money; if you winnin' you takin' de girls upstairs."

"Is dat so?" laughed Mbozi. "What chance dey got of winnin' a rubber against great pair like us? Even de stupid white-Bwanas wouldn't bettin' on it."

0–0–0

That evening at ten o'clock Mbozi and the Witchdoctor arrived at the Zengali Wildcat Club. Both were immaculately attired. The Witchdoctor was wearing a vulture-feathered headdress that he normally reserved for special occasions such as circumcisions and fertility rites. Mbozi had somehow acquired a western suit in a blue pinstripe. Business at the club was brisk and almost half the tables were in play. Some of the remaining tables were occupied by pairs of girls, waiting for customers. Others were apparently unattended.

"Hah!" exclaimed Mbozi excitedly. "See de empty tables? Some of de girls mus' have jus' had de misfortune to losin' a rubber."

"You young lads fancy a game?" enquired a none-too-youthful female at one of the tables by the door.

Mbozi moved forward eagerly but the Witchdoctor grabbed his shoulder. "Dey's not too hot lookin'," he said. "Particularly de one you would endin' up with."

"Yeah, but dis table only 25 mpengos a 100," replied Mbozi. "And I bet dey can't playin' at all."

"Dem old hags mos' probably losin' de rubber on purpose when I sittin' down at de table," declared the Witchdoctor. He dragged Mbozi to a table near the staircase where two stylish twenty-year-olds were in attendance. "What's de stakes here?" he enquired, licking his lips.

"Dis de top table. We play for 300 mpengos a 100," replied Leila,
the taller of the two girls. "You handsome guys like to takin' us on?"

Mbozi and the Witchdoctor needed no further enticement. They
took their seats and the rubber commenced.

Love all
Dealer West

```
              ♠ K J 4
              ♡ K 10 9 2
              ◇ A 10 3
              ♣ A 9 5
♠ Q 10 5         N          ♠ 7
♡ J 7 3       W     E       ♡ Q 8 6 5
◇ Q 8 6          S          ◇ K 9 4 2
♣ K Q J 3                   ♣ 10 7 6 4
              ♠ A 9 8 6 3 2
              ♡ A 4
              ◇ J 7 5
              ♣ 8 2
```

South	West	North	East
Leila	Witch-doctor	Waheda	Mbozi
—	No	1♡	No
1♠	No	1NT	No
4♠	End		

The two girls reached four spades in quick time and the
Witchdoctor made the obvious lead of the king of clubs. The young
declarer, who was clad in a tasteful white cocktail dress, ducked the
opening lead. No switch suggested itself, so the Witchdoctor
continued with the queen of clubs at trick two.

Leila won in the dummy and ruffed a third round of clubs with the
♠ 9. She then cashed the ace of trumps and finessed the jack, East
showing out. After this manoeuvre she could count six trump tricks
and four winners in the side suits. The game could not be beaten.

The Witchdoctor stared curiously at the young declarer who was
smiling prettily at her partner. Why had she finessed in the trump
suit? It occurred to him that she would have made the contract even if
the finesse had lost. Her red suits were good enough to guarantee an
extra trick whatever East returned. After a heart return to the jack
and king, for example, declarer would cash the ace of hearts and
return to dummy with the king of trumps. She would then be able to

discard one diamond on ♡ 10 and subsequently another one on ♡ 9.

Had she known what she was doing? The Witchdoctor shook his head. No, she probably always finessed against the queen when there were four cards out.

A hand or two later the two house players bid to a small slam in hearts. The Witchdoctor, who was on lead, stared grimly at his hand. If the slam succeeded, the rubber would more or less clean them out. This was the deal:

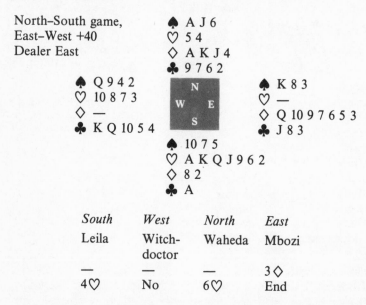

North–South game,
East–West +40
Dealer East

North
♠ A J 6
♡ 5 4
◇ A K J 4
♣ 9 7 6 2

West
♠ Q 9 4 2
♡ 10 8 7 3
◇ —
♣ K Q 10 5 4

East
♠ K 8 3
♡ —
◇ Q 10 9 7 6 5 3
♣ J 8 3

South
♠ 10 7 5
♡ A K Q J 9 6 2
◇ 8 2
♣ A

South	West	North	East
Leila	Witch-doctor	Waheda	Mbozi
—	—	—	3◇
4♡	No	6♡	End

The Witchdoctor spun the king of clubs onto the table. Leila won with the ace and drew trumps in four rounds, discarding two diamonds from the table. She then played a spade to the jack and king. It seemed to Mbozi, sitting East, that declarer might well hold Q x of spades and a doubleton club. He fired back a club, which was ruffed by declarer.

Leila now cashed the ace-king of diamonds and ruffed another club, killing East's guard in the suit. When she played her last trump the Witchdoctor was caught in this simple ending:

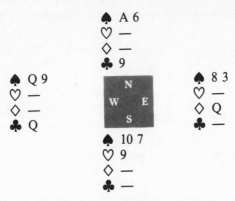

```
              ♠ A 6
              ♡ —
              ◇ —
              ♣ 9
♠ Q 9                        ♠ 8 3
♡ —         N               ♡ —
◇ —      W     E            ◇ Q
♣ Q         S               ♣ —
              ♠ 10 7
              ♡ 9
              ◇ —
              ♣ —
```

Hoping for the best, the Witchdoctor threw a spade but Leila now claimed two spade tricks for her contract.

"Well, you two gentlemen sure playin' a fine game," said Waheda, a slender beauty from the Nahumid tribe. "Jus' bad luck we gettin' all de cards dat time. 18 points, I makin' it. Dat's 5400 mpengos."

Mbozi and the Witchdoctor saw no alternative but to pay up. They then made hastily for the bar, declining the offer of a further rubber.

"Bafaqhassar!" exclaimed Mbozi. "I's almost cleaned out already. How much you got left?"

The Witchdoctor ordered two glasses of Zbolwumba brandy from the dowdy barmaid, then turned to inspect the contents of his wallet. "1800 mpengos, dat's all," he replied. "Have to movin' to de cheaper tables."

The barmaid, whose dress seemed at least one size too small for her, placed the brandies on the counter. "Two doubles," she said. "Dat'll be 1400 mpengos, not includin' de service."

The Witchdoctor rolled his eyes in disbelief as he handed over the money. 1400 mpengos? He wouldn't be returning to this establishment in a hurry.

"You butcherin' de defence on dat last one," he said, glaring at Mbozi over the rim of his brandy glass. "You should returnin' a spade when you gettin' in. Dat breakin' up de squeeze."

"If my defence ain't good enough for you," replied Mbozi fiercely, "you can bringin' someone else next time."

"Hah! Who you got in mind?" exclaimed the Witchdoctor. "White bwanas wouldn't be seen dead in dis place." He took a mouthful of brandy and swilled it round his mouth in disgusting fashion. "Not much point in de Parrot-bird comin' either," he added. "He wouldn't knowin' what to do if he winnin' a rubber."

Mbozi cast his mind back to the heart slam once more. "Declarer cockin' up de play, anyhow," he said. "She should keepin' ◊ A K J in dummy and leadin' de ten of spades. You have to coverin' and after de trumps are run I gettin' endplayed with de other spade to lead into de diamonds."

"Dat's right, a strip-squeeze," agreed the Witchdoctor. "Dey should knowin' all about dat play in club like dis." He drained his glass. "I's feelin' better after dat," he declared. "You ready for another rubber?"

"Against de old hags by de door?" replied Mbozi. "No, let's go."

"I was thinkin' of another rubber against dem two we jus' played," said the Witchdoctor, a glint in his eye. "Don' believe we could possibly losin' two rubbers against couple of young girls."

A foolish grin came to Mbozi's face. "Yeah. Sure would be great to get dem two upstairs," he said. "If we do losin' we just' gonna have to run for it."

Strolling confidently to the top table, Mbozi and the Witchdoctor resumed their seats. A short while later this deal occurred:

Love all,
East–West +60
Dealer South

	♠ Q 9 7 6 4 3 2	
	♡ J 7 2	
	◊ 10 2	
	♣ A	
♠ A	N	♠ —
♡ 9 8 6 3	W E	♡ Q 5 4
◊ K 9 4	S	◊ J 8 7 5 3
♣ J 10 8 7 6		♣ K Q 5 4 2
	♠ K J 10 8 5	
	♡ A K 10	
	◊ A Q 6	
	♣ 9 3	

South	West	North	East
Witch- doctor	Leila	Mbozi	Waheda
1 ♠	No	4 ♣	dble
4NT	No	5 ◊	No
6 ♠	End		

Mbozi's four club call showed a sound raise to game with a club control. The Witchdoctor needed no further encouragement to bid the slam. Since the stakes were high he made a Blackwood call on the way, a mechanism he usually neglected.

Leila's impeccably manicured fingers hovered over her cards, eventually selecting the jack of clubs as her opening lead. The Witchdoctor won in dummy, observing that Mbozi had little to spare for his bid. If both red suit finesses were right the contract was cold. If both were wrong there was no hope. The critical case was when just one of the finesses was right. The Witchdoctor surveyed his cards thoughtfully. Yes, he would have to start by eliminating the red suit where the finesse was onside. He could then ruff his remaining club and exit in trumps. With any luck West would win and have to play into the other red suit.

How could he tell which red suit finesse was right? In an effort to discover, he led the jack of hearts from dummy at trick two. Waheda was unimpressed by this card. She followed at an even pace with ♡ 4.

Deciding that the heart queen was probably offside, the Witchdoctor put up the ace and returned to dummy with a club ruff. He then switched his attack to the diamond suit, finessing the queen. This line of play was not a success. West won with the king, cashed the trump ace and exited in diamonds. The Witchdoctor was not amused to find that the heart finesse had been right all the time. If he had run the jack of hearts, the contract could have been made.

"You didn't coverin' de jack of hearts?" he queried, leering at the beauty in the East seat.

Waheda smiled back in friendly fashion. "If you wantin' soft defences all de time, you should playin' on de 25 mpengo tables by de door," she said. She turned to her partner. "Shouldn't you leadin' de ace of trumps, Leila?"

"Yeah, dat's right," replied Leila, giving a delicate little yawn. "Didn't costin', fortunately."

The score had advanced to Game All when the Witchdoctor, sitting South, picked up this hand:

♠ Q 10 8 7 6 2
♡ Q 4
◊ 10 8 6 4
♣ 5

"Three clubs," said Waheda, in front of him.
"Pass," said the Witchdoctor reluctantly.
"Three no-trumps," said Leila.

Two passes followed and the Witchdoctor's heart sank as he surveyed his four-count. Surely this was the end of the rubber. Something very nasty would happen if they couldn't pay up and were caught trying to make their escape.

"Four spades," said the Witchdoctor, before he could stop himself.
"Double!" said Leila.

No further bidding resulted. This was the full deal:

Game all
Dealer East

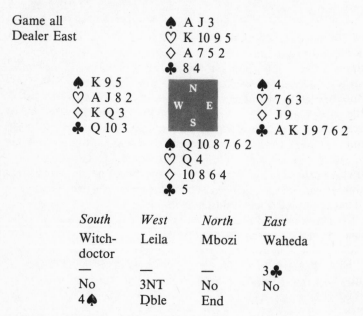

♠ A J 3
♡ K 10 9 5
◇ A 7 5 2
♣ 8 4

♠ K 9 5
♡ A J 8 2
◇ K Q 3
♣ Q 10 3

♠ 4
♡ 7 6 3
◇ J 9
♣ A K J 9 7 6 2

♠ Q 10 8 7 6 2
♡ Q 4
◇ 10 8 6 4
♣ 5

South	West	North	East
Witch-doctor	Leila	Mbozi	Waheda
—	—	—	3♣
No	3NT	No	No
4♠	Dble	End	

Leila led ♣ 3 to her partner's king and the ace of clubs was continued. The Witchdoctor ruffed and ran the ♠ 10 successfully. Next he played a spade to the jack and cashed the ace of spades, removing the defenders' trumps. A heart to the queen and ace left Leila on lead. Not giving the matter much thought, she exited safely with a club. The Witchdoctor ruffed and led the last trump to this end position:

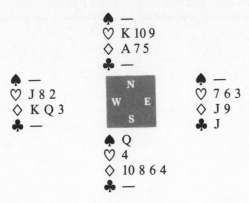

♠ —
♡ K 10 9
◇ A 7 5
♣ —

♠ —   ♠ —
♡ J 8 2   ♡ 7 6 3
◇ K Q 3   ◇ J 9
♣ —   ♣ J

♠ Q
♡ 4
◇ 10 8 6 4
♣ —

Leila had no answer to the last trump. If she discarded a heart,
dummy would score three tricks in the suit. If she tried a low diamond
instead, declarer would easily be able to establish his diamonds
without letting East into the lead to cash her club. In desperation
Leila decided to throw the queen of diamonds. The Witchdoctor
discarded a heart from dummy and continued with a low diamond
from hand. When Leila put in the king he ducked the trick. Dummy's
ace won the diamond return, dropping East's jack, and the
Witchdoctor cashed two more diamond tricks and the king of hearts,
wrapping up the contract.

The Witchdoctor rose triumphantly to his feet. "I think I deservin'
de first choice after dat," he declared. Pointing a gnarled finger at
Leila, he turned towards the staircase.

"Just a minute," called Leila. "We ain't paid you yet."

"Hah! You do de payin' upstairs," exclaimed the Witchdoctor
with relish. "You won't forget losin' dis rubber in a hurry."

"Nor will dis little beauty," said Mbozi, sweeping Waheda into his
arms.

"Bouncers!" squealed Waheda, struggling vigorously to free
herself.

Two barrel-chested members of the Zbolwumba tribe appeared
from nowhere. They grabbed Mbozi and the Witchdoctor by the
collar, carried them through the back exit and dumped them into the
yard outside. "If you loony-boys showin' your faces here again you
won' livin' to regret it," declared one of the bouncers. "Dis
respectable club here."

The two strong-arm men disappeared, slamming the door behind them. Mbozi and the Witchdoctor were left looking up at the stars.

"Who tellin' you dis place a brothel-hut?" said Mbozi. "Don' seemin' like one to me."

"Who do you think?" replied the Witchdoctor, flashing his eyes malevolently. "Dat Parrot-bird mos' probably laughin' his head off at us comin' all dis way for nothin'."

Mbozi rose painfully to his feet and brushed the dust off his pinstripe trousers. "He laughin' on de other side of his beak when I gettin' hold of him," he said.

15

The Parrot's Accusation

Walking past the fires where the Bozwambi womenfolk were busy preparing the evening meal, Brother Tobias made his way towards the Parrot's hut – an airy residence thatched with banana palm.

"Anyone at home?" he called, ducking through the doorway.

When his eyes became accustomed to the darkness, Brother Tobias could see the Parrot on his usual perch in the far corner. He was in a sorry state. His plumage was in disarray, he had a painful-looking black eye and his right wing was tied in a splint.

"Good gracious!" exclaimed Brother Tobias. "You look like something the cat brought home. How on earth did that happen?"

"A practical joke misfired, that's all," croaked the Parrot. "Haven't any aspirin on you, have you?"

"A practical joke?" said Brother Tobias. "Do you mean that some member of our community found it a source of amusement to rough you up like this?"

"Actually it was a small joke I played on someone else," replied the Parrot. "Mbozi and the Witchdoctor have no sense of humour, that's the trouble."

Brother Tobias gave a sympathetic shake of the head. It was well known that anyone who crossed the Witchdoctor's path paid heavily for the privilege. "If you fancy a spot of revenge, we could take them on at tonight's partnership game" he suggested. "They'd be too proud to refuse a 100 mpengo game. A few big rubbers in our favour would soon put them in their place."

Not long afterwards the Bozwambi partnership evening was well under way. Five or six tables were playing at the usual stakes of 10 mpengos-a-100, and in the centre of the hut the Witchdoctor and Mbozi were doing battle with the Parrot and Brother Tobias. The first two rubbers had been shared and the third rubber had just reached Game All. Brother Tobias, sitting West, leaned forward and picked up these cards:

♠ 10 9 7 2
♡ Q J 8 3
◇ J 10 5
♣ A 8

The Parrot, sitting East, opened with a multi-coloured two diamonds, a convention that was allowed at rubber bridge only on partnership nights.

"Four clubs," said the Witchdoctor, who was attired – smartly for him – in a white djellaba studded with black beads.

Brother Tobias passed and Mbozi, who was North, emerged with a Blackwood 4NT. The Parrot passed and the Witchdoctor bid five diamonds, showing one ace.

Mbozi gave a sullen glance at his partner and sat back in his chair. It was obvious to all at the table that two aces were missing. "Six clubs," he said.

This call was passed out and Brother Tobias surveyed his cards once more. It seemed that a lot of points – and prestige – might hang on his choice of opening lead. Which ace did partner hold? Since Brother Tobias had two heart honours himself, it seemed more likely that the Parrot's multi was based on a spade suit. He therefore decided to lead ♠ 10. This was the full deal:

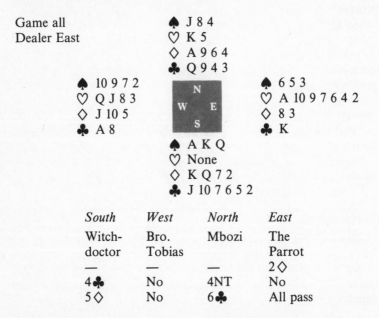

Game all
Dealer East

		♠ J 8 4	
		♡ K 5	
		◇ A 9 6 4	
		♣ Q 9 4 3	

♠ 10 9 7 2			♠ 6 5 3
♡ Q J 8 3		N	♡ A 10 9 7 6 4 2
◇ J 10 5	W	E	◇ 8 3
♣ A 8		S	♣ K

		♠ A K Q	
		♡ None	
		◇ K Q 7 2	
		♣ J 10 7 6 5 2	

South	West	North	East
Witch-	Bro.	Mbozi	The
doctor	Tobias		Parrot
—	—	—	2◇
4♣	No	4NT	No
5◇	No	6♣	All pass

The ♠ 10 produced the 4, 3 and ace. Brother Tobias could feel his heart pounding. Obviously the Parrot's bid was based on a six-card heart suit. Was there any way that declarer could get rid of his heart loser?

The Witchdoctor gave his customary disgusting sniff as he surveyed the dummy. How could he encourage the defenders to crash their trump honours? The Parrot was too good a player to cover the queen of clubs from a doubleton honour. It must be better odds to play for an indiscretion from Brother Tobias.

Before playing on trumps the Witchdoctor made the cunning deceptive move of cashing the king–queen of diamonds. He then led a low trump from hand.

Brother Tobias could not believe his good fortune. Obviously declarer was trying to sneak an entry to dummy to discard his heart loser on the ace of diamonds. With a triumphant flick of the wrist he tossed the ace of clubs onto the table. When the king of clubs fell from the Parrot, the Witchdoctor cackled with laughter and faced his hand, claiming the contract.

"You idiot!" shrieked the Parrot, jumping on the table and striding towards Brother Tobias. "You great BUFFOON!"

"But I thought the king–queen of diamonds were doubleton," protested Brother Tobias. "You played high–low in diamonds, so obviously I put you with four."

The Parrot shook his head in disbelief, muttering a swearword.

"Anyhow," continued Brother Tobias, "no-one but a raving lunatic would jump to the four level on a jack-high suit. How could I possibly imagine I would crash the trump honours?"

"Which diamonds did I play?" demanded the Parrot, flapping his left wing in agitated fashion.

"I've no idea," replied Brother Tobias. "You played high–low. That's all that matters."

"I played the 8, then the 3," persisted the Parrot. "Would I choose those cards from a holding of 8–7–3–2?"

"I don't see why not," declared Brother Tobias.

"Nine," said the Witchdoctor.

"What?" said Brother Tobias, spinning round angrily.

"Nine points, de rubber," said the Witchdoctor, tapping his scorepad. "Nine hundred mpengos to pay."

No other partnerships were willing to cut into such a high stake game, so the same four embarked on a new rubber. This was the first hand:

Love all
Dealer East

```
                    ♠ K 8 4
                    ♡ A Q 9
                    ◇ 8 5 4
                    ♣ 8 7 6 2
♠ 6                                  ♠ Q 10 9 7 5 2
♡ 10 8 6 5 2          N              ♡ 7 3
◇ A K 7           W     E            ◇ Q 6 3
♣ J 10 4 3           S              ♣ Q 9
                    ♠ A J 3
                    ♡ K J 4
                    ◇ J 10 9 2
                    ♣ A K 5
```

South	West	North	East
Witch-	Bro.	Mbozi	The
doctor	Tobias		Parrot
—	—	—	2◇
2NT	No	3NT	All pass

Once more the Parrot opened with a multi-coloured two diamond call. The Witchdoctor was soon in 3NT and Brother Tobias paused to consider his opening lead.

The Parrot's opening bid was obviously based on spades, but would he have the entries to get the suit going? It seemed unlikely, so Brother Tobias decided to attack in his own suit. The ♡ 5 lead was won by dummy's 9 and the Witchdoctor continued with a low diamond to the jack and king.

There was obviously no future in hearts, so Brother Tobias switched to a low club. The queen came from the Parrot and the Witchdoctor ducked the trick. The contract was now safe. It made no difference whether the Parrot returned a heart or a club. When he subsequently gained the lead with the queen of diamonds he would have no cards remaining in the key suit. In practice, the Parrot decided to return ♣ 9. The Witchdoctor won with the ace and eventually established a trick for himself in diamonds. The marked spade finesse then gave him nine tricks.

"Mos' excellent play, partner," exclaimed a well-pleased Mbozi. "You in de soup bucket for sure if you don' duckin' de first round of clubs."

"Yeah, dat weren't too difficult," replied the Witchdoctor. "Once de Parrot-bird don' winnin' de first diamond, I's always OK."

Brother Tobias blinked, then leaned forward in his seat. "Put up your queen of diamonds and declarer's a doomed man," he said. "We come to our heart tricks before he can establish a diamond."

The Parrot gave a nod of the beak, accepting that this was true. "A difficult defence to find at the best of times," he observed. "Quite impossible when you've been put through the mangle like I have."

"Yes, that reminds me," said Brother Tobias, turning towards the Witchdoctor and giving him a fiery glance. "Is it true that you and Mbozi are responsible for the Parrot's present condition?"

"Hah! You don' know what he doin' to us," replied Mbozi. "He deservin' everythin' he got."

"Dat's right," agreed the Witchdoctor. "Mind you, it weren't us what doin' it. Mus' have been some friends of ours who hearin' what he done to us."

"Don't be ridiculous," replied Brother Tobias. "The Parrot has positively identified you as the two intruders who broke into his hut last night."

"Parrot-bird lyin' through beak as usual," said the Witchdoctor, giving the Parrot a scornful look. "Anyhow, why you takin' his word for what happened? Don' expect he could even seein' properly with black eye like dat!"

16

Father Gregory's Potion

The Bozwambi team had so far encountered little opposition in the Bhumpopo Gold Cup. In the fourth round, which was no longer regionalized, they had been drawn against a team from Potuzzi, a suburb of Bhumpopo City. Since Potuzzi was well over 100 miles away, the match was to be played at a half-way venue, a mission hall in the settlement of Kah-Entrebba.

"Ah, welcome, welcome!" said Father Gregory, the elderly leader of the mission. "Your opponents aren't here yet. Can I tempt you to a cup of English tea?"

"That would be a rare treat," replied Brother Tobias, dismounting from the elephant with some difficulty. "The Bozwambi tribe make some concoction from mulberry leaves, but it's nothing like the real thing."

Beckoning everyone to follow him into the mission hut, Father Gregory produced a king-size pack of Brooke Bond tea bags. Ten minutes later everyone was presented with a large cup of tea.

Brother Tobias winced as he took his first mouthful. What a disappointment! It tasted watery and rather bitter, scarcely an improvement on the mulberry stuff.

"Of course you can't buy tea like this over here," said Father Gregory, gazing fondly into his cup. "I brought a supply with me when we first established this mission. I save it for special occasions."

Brother Tobias glanced at the packet of tea bags. On the side of the carton he could just make out the words 'BEST BEFORE JAN 69'.

A jeep pulled up outside the mission hut. Father Gregory leapt to his feet and out into the sunlight. "Welcome to Kah-Entrebba," he said. "Arduous drive from Potuzzi, isn't it? You must have some English tea before you start."

"Mos' kind of you," replied Adel Bahadj, the visiting team's captain, "But we don' usually takin' stimulants before a big game. Shall we startin' straight away?"

"No, no. Out of the question, " said Brother Tobias, appearing at the doorway of the hut. "You must have some tea first." It was only fair, he thought, that both teams should incur the same penalty.

The match had not been long under way when the Parrot's defence was put to the test.

North–South game
Dealer East

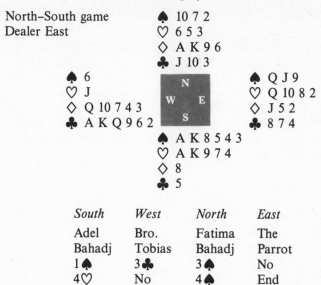

```
              ♠ 10 7 2
              ♡ 6 5 3
              ◇ A K 9 6
              ♣ J 10 3
♠ 6                              ♠ Q J 9
♡ J              N               ♡ Q 10 8 2
◇ Q 10 7 4 3   W   E             ◇ J 5 2
♣ A K Q 9 6 2     S              ♣ 8 7 4
              ♠ A K 8 5 4 3
              ♡ A K 9 7 4
              ◇ 8
              ♣ 5
```

South	*West*	*North*	*East*
Adel	Bro.	Fatima	The
Bahadj	Tobias	Bahadj	Parrot
1♠	3♣	3♠	No
4♡	No	4♠	End

Adel Bahadj considered making one more slam invitation over four spades, eventually deciding against it. When the ace of clubs was led and dummy appeared, he nodded approvingly. Yes, twelve tricks would be quite impossible on a club lead.

At trick 2 Brother Tobias played another club honour. Declarer ruffed and cashed the ace and king of trumps. When West showed out, Adel Bahadj realised for the first time that even ten tricks might be in danger. If East held four hearts he would be able to win the third round of hearts, draw dummy's last trump and cash another heart trick.

Mr. Bahadj stroked his chin thoughtfully. It seemed he could avoid this fate by ducking the first round of hearts to West, who would have no trump to play back. With this in mind, he crossed to the ace of diamonds and led a low heart.

The Parrot had a good picture of declarer's hand at this stage. His partner had played the 3 on the first round of diamonds, suggesting an odd number. It looked as though South, who had bid spades and hearts, was 6–5–1–1. If his hearts were as good as A K J x x, nothing could be done. If his hearts were any weaker, though, it seemed the Parrot could not lose by inserting the queen on this trick. Leaning towards the wooden card holder, he extracted the queen of hearts with his beak and tossed it on the table. Mr. Bahadj won the trick with the ace, the jack falling from West.

When the king of hearts was cashed, West showed out. Playing another heart from hand would obviously lead to defeat, so Mr. Bahadj threw East in with the queen of trumps, hoping for a red suit return. When the Parrot was able to exit safely in clubs declarer had to concede two more heart tricks. He was one down.

"You's big man, Adel," remarked Mrs. Bahadj, "but I don't think you makin' de best of dat one."

Mr. Bahadj glared at his wife. "Pity you weren't playing it, my beloved," he said, with heavy sarcasm. "What line of play did you havin' in mind?"

"Well, I didn't seein' exactly what cards you had," replied Mrs. Bahadj. "But I's sure you should makin' it, all de same."

Brother Tobias leaned forward. "I think your wife means that you should have cashed the ace and king of hearts before drawing a second round of trumps," he said. "That guarantees the contract, even if the king of hearts gets ruffed."

"Dat's what I's thinkin', too," declared Mrs. Bahadj, sitting back in her chair. "Are you listenin', Adel? Play de top hearts first and you mus' makin' it."

At the other end of the mission hall Mbozi and the Witchdoctor were facing earnest opponents, two third-year medical students from Bhumpopo City University. Father Gregory, still nursing a cup of tea, was watching the play.

Love all
Dealer South

	♠ A J 6 5	
	♡ 8 7 4	
	◇ K 6 4	
	♣ A 7 2	

♠ Q 10 7 2		♠ K 9 8 3
♡ K J 6 5 2	N	♡ Q 9
◇ A J 9	W E	◇ 10 7 3 2
♣ Q	S	♣ J 10 4

	♠ 4	
	♡ A 10 3	
	◇ Q 8 5	
	♣ K 9 8 6 5 3	

South	West	North	East
Witch-	Abdah	Mbozi	Steven
doctor	Kelim		Mkomo
No	1♡	Dble	No
3♣	End		

Abdah Kelim led a low spade against three clubs and the Witchdoctor won with dummy's ace. He then ruffed a spade and exited with ♡ 3. Father Gregory watched these strange manoeuvres in amazement. What on earth was declarer up to? With nine trumps between the hands and no ruffs to be taken in the dummy it surely must be right to draw trumps first. Still, thought Father Gregory, one shouldn't criticize. It was amazing that these natives could play the game at all.

East won the heart trick with the 9 and returned the queen of hearts to the ace. The Witchdoctor now cashed the king and ace of clubs, revealing a trump loser. He then ruffed a third round of spades, leaving these cards at large:

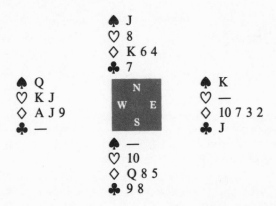

```
              ♠ J
              ♡ 8
              ◇ K 6 4
              ♣ 7
 ♠ Q          ┌─────────┐       ♠ K
 ♡ K J        │   N     │       ♡ —
 ◇ A J 9      │ W     E │       ◇ 10 7 3 2
 ♣ —          │   S     │       ♣ J
              └─────────┘
              ♠ —
              ♡ 10
              ◇ Q 8 5
              ♣ 9 8
```

The Witchdoctor played a diamond to the king and ruffed dummy's last spade. When West was thrown in with a heart, he found he was endplayed. A heart return would give a ruff-and-discard and a diamond would allow declarer's queen to score. The Witchdoctor faced his cards, claiming nine tricks.

Father Gregory shook his head in amazement and made a mental note to study the hand later. Declarer had started the hand with five certain losers, but one of them seemed to have vanished somehow. Perhaps those strange plays at the start of the hand had made a difference after all.

The Bozwambi team were a comfortable 42 IMPs ahead when the half-time comparison was made. There seemed to be every prospect of forcing an early concession as the second half started.

The Witchdoctor was soon in action again.

Game all
Dealer East

♠ —
♡ K 9 7 6 4 2
♢ A 8 5 3 2
♣ 7 4

♠ A 2
♡ Q 10 5
♢ K Q J 6
♣ K Q 10 9

♠ K Q J 10 8 6 5 3
♡ J 3
♢ 10 9 4
♣ —

♠ 9 7 4
♡ A 8
♢ 7
♣ A J 8 6 5 3 2

South	West	North	East
Witch-	Mrs.	Mbozi	Mr.
doctor	Bahadj		Bahadj
—	—	—	4♠
5♣	Dble	End	

Mr. Bahadj opened four spades and the Witchdoctor made a rather wild overcall of five clubs.

"Double!" said Mrs. Bahadj, trusting that this call would meet with her husband's approval.

Mbozi passed and Adel Bahadj thumbed through his cards once more. Would Fatima have enough in the red suits to make five spades a good bet?

Mrs. Bahadj gave her husband a sharp glance. If he took her out of this particular double he could sleep in the spare room tonight.

"No bid," said Mr. Bahadj.

Mrs. Bahadj led the king of diamonds, won by dummy's ace. The Witchdoctor ruffed a diamond in hand, ruffed a spade, then ruffed another diamond. Crossing to dummy with a second spade ruff, he ruffed yet another diamond, East discarding a spade. Mr. Bahadj was observing the path of the play with increasing distaste. Surely Fatima would have done better to lead a trump?

The Witchdoctor cleared his throat in grotesque fashion, then cashed the ace and king of hearts and ruffed a heart in hand. The position now was:

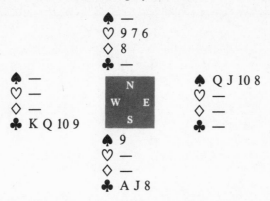

The Witchdoctor, who had so far not lost a trick, exited with ♠ 9. Mrs. Bahadj ruffed the trick and played back the king of trumps. With a gap-toothed leer in her direction the Witchdoctor followed with the 8 of trumps. He then faced his trump tenace, claiming the contract.

"What a lead, Fatima!" exclaimed Mr. Bahadj. "Lead de king of trumps and we mus' takin' 500. He losin' three trump tricks and a spade, however he playin' it."

"Don't be ridiculous, Adel," retorted Mrs. Bahadj. "Leading from K Q J is recommended in all de bridge books." She shook her head sadly, embarrassed at her husband's ignorance. "It's de second best lead after A K Q," she continued. "Ain't you never seen a table of de best leads?"

"Yes, silly of me, forgettin' dat," replied Mr. Bahadj with ponderous irony. "It was very clever lead, my dearest. Mos' unlucky to costin' 1250 points, I mus' say."

With thirty-two of the forty-eight boards played, the Bozwambi team had established a lead of 77 IMPs. Brother Tobias walked over to the opponents' table. "Long drive back to Bhumpopo City, isn't it?" he said. "Would an early finish suit you?"

"Not unless your team is concedin' de match," replied Mr. Bahadj stiffly. "Don't see why our luck shouldn't changin' in de last two sets."

"Quite right; a lot can happenin' in sixteen boards," said Mrs. Bahadj, agreeing with her husband for the first time in the match. "One of de opposin' team might gettin' bitten by a snake, or mebbe gettin' nasty attack of food poisonin'."

Brother Tobias was unamused. "In that case we'd be fortunate indeed that you have two medical students in your team," he replied. "I'm sure they would revive us. Shall we restart?"

North–South game
Dealer West

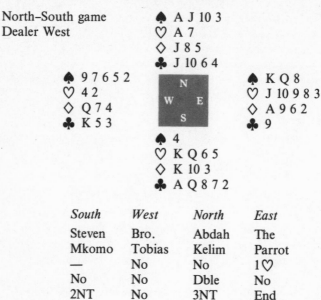

♠ A J 10 3
♡ A 7
◇ J 8 5
♣ J 10 6 4

♠ 9 7 6 5 2
♡ 4 2
◇ Q 7 4
♣ K 5 3

♠ K Q 8
♡ J 10 9 8 3
◇ A 9 6 2
♣ 9

♠ 4
♡ K Q 6 5
◇ K 10 3
♣ A Q 8 7 2

South	West	North	East
Steven	Bro.	Abdah	The
Mkomo	Tobias	Kelim	Parrot
—	No	No	1♡
No	No	Dble	No
2NT	No	3NT	End

The Parrot made a somewhat light opening in the third seat but the students brushed this aside, quickly reaching 3NT. Brother Tobias, who had two possible cards of re-entry, decided to attack in spades rather than in hearts. This was a courageous manoeuvre. The Parrot was not known for his sympathetic attitude to partners who gave away game swings by leading their own suit instead of his.

Mkomo played the jack of spades from dummy at trick 1, the Parrot winning with the queen. A low diamond switch went to Brother Tobias's queen and back came ◇ 7. The jack was played from dummy, but the Parrot was not to be tempted. Resolutely retaining his ace of diamonds, he allowed dummy's jack to win the trick.

Declarer made the obvious move now of a club finesse, which lost to West's king. Thanks to the Parrot's hold-up in diamonds the defenders could now cash two tricks in the suit, putting the contract one down.

"Just as well I didn't lead your suit," remarked Brother Tobias. "It's an easy make on a heart lead."

The Parrot muttered something, then reached out a claw for his scorecard.

"Why don't you open your beak when you speak?" said Brother Tobias. "We might be able to catch the odd word, then."

"I SAID IT'S AN EASY MAKE ON A SPADE LEAD, TOO!"
screeched the Parrot, his patience exhausted.

Brother Tobias winced and turned apologetically to the two
opponents. "I hope you'll excuse that outbreak," he said. "My
colleague, Brother Luke, holds classes in etiquette, but my partner
has so far refused to attend."

In the other room the Witchdoctor arrived in the same contract:

South	West	North	East
Witch-	Mrs.	Mbozi	Mr.
doctor	Bahadj		Bahadj
—	No	No	1♡
2♣	No	2♡	No
3NT	End		

Mrs. Bahadj, who made it a policy to lead her husband's suit as
rarely as possible, led a spade against 3NT.

"Ace," barked the Witchdoctor as soon as dummy went down.
"An' de club jack."

The finesse lost to the king but the defenders were powerless.
Doing the best she could, West returned a spade to East's queen and a
low diamond was played back. Placing the ace with the opening bid,
the Witchdoctor put up the king successfully. Nine tricks were there.

With one set of eight boards remaining, the Bozwambi team's lead
had stretched to an embarrassing 103 IMPs. Summoning a cheery
smile, Brother Tobias approached the opponents' table once more.

"Yes?" said Mr. Bahadj. "You wantin' somethin'?"

"Er, well . . . I was just wondering if you. . ." Brother Tobias
paused to search for the right words. "What I mean is . . . there don't
seem to be many snakes around."

"Mebbe we should playin' de last set in de long grass outside?"
suggested Mr. Bahadj sternly.

Suddenly he stood up, chuckling to himself. He stretched out a
hand towards Brother Tobias. "Only jokin'. We's had enough, now,"
he said. "We was jus' wonderin' if we could makin' our escape
without Father Gregory seein' us. Couldn't facin' another cup of dat
awful tea."

"Unbelievable stuff, wasn't it?" agreed Brother Tobias. "Did you
see the packet it came from? It had a date of 1969 on it."

"Ah, you've finished. What excellent timing!" came a jovial voice
from across the room. "You must come along to my hut for a little
farewell treat. No, I insist. The pot's just brewed."

PART III

St. Titus at the Spring Foursomes

17

Setting up Base Camp

The Abbot pulled his ancient Austin Seven to a halt and peered through the windscreen. "This must be it," he said. "Ah yes, there's a sign – *The Charitable Brothers of Bartholomew.*"

The Abbot parked his car and the four monks approached the weather-worn front door of the establishment. The Abbot had scarcely rung the bell when the door creaked open.

"Abbot Hugo?" said the elderly friar at the door.

"Yes, indeed," replied the Abbot heartily. "Delighted to meet you. Is my car all right over there?"

The friar peered round the door. "Well, perhaps you might move it forward a foot or two," he replied. "I put some chrysanthemum seeds in that bed last week."

The four visitors were soon enjoying a cup of tea with Father Bertram, leader of the order and a direct descendant of Brother Bartholomew.

"We receive very few callers here," he informed them. "We were most excited to hear of your intended visit."

"Hmm, these are excellent rock cakes," mumbled the Abbot. "Very fresh."

"We've arranged a full programme for your visit," continued Father Bertram. "Tomorrow evening Brother Gordon's madrigal ensemble will be entertaining us, and the following morning I thought we might. . ."

"That's most kind of you but I regret we shall be unavailable," replied the Abbot. "Didn't I mention, it in my letter? We're all playing in the Spring Foursomes, just down the road at Eastbourne."

"Playing?" queried Father Bertram. "Playing what?"

"Er . . . bridge," replied the Abbot, reaching for another cake and finding that the plate was empty. "I looked you up in the Yellow Pages. You were the nearest monastic establishment to Eastbourne."

"I see," said Father Bertram, rising sternly to his feet. "The matter was certainly not made clear in your letter. Please excuse me while I inform Brother Gordon's ensemble that they are rehearsing to no purpose."

After a disappointing lunch in the Brotherhood's spartan dining hall, the monastery team headed towards the Grand Hotel for the first round of the Spring Foursomes. As usual, the Abbot drove at breakneck speed, showing little concern for the two monks sitting at the back of the car.

"Do you think they normally eat as poorly as that?" said the Abbot, just beating an invalid carriage to a vacant parking space.

"Perhaps they were trying to impress us with their austerity," replied Brother Lucius. "I must say, I've never had sprout soup as a main course before."

As they approached the front steps of the hotel Brother Xavier moved ahead, eager to see who their first opponents would be.

"Brother Xavier!" called the Abbot sharply. "No need to behave like an impetuous schoolboy. I don't suppose we shall be unduly extended in the early rounds."

The four monks entered the hotel and the Abbot strolled nonchalantly towards the board that was displaying the draw. He scanned the list and soon spotted *Yorke-Smith v Parker*. Parker? Never heard of him, thought the Abbot.

The monastery team's opponents turned out to be some students from a West London polytechnic. The first half was closely contested, the Abbot's team taking the lead by 8 IMPs. This hand arrived midway through the second half.

Love all
Dealer North

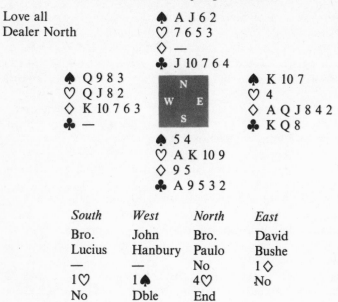

```
                    ♠ A J 6 2
                    ♡ 7 6 5 3
                    ◇ —
                    ♣ J 10 7 6 4
   ♠ Q 9 8 3              ♠ K 10 7
   ♡ Q J 8 2       N      ♡ 4
   ◇ K 10 7 6 3  W   E    ◇ A Q J 8 4 2
   ♣ —            S       ♣ K Q 8
                    ♠ 5 4
                    ♡ A K 10 9
                    ◇ 9 5
                    ♣ A 9 5 3 2
```

South	West	North	East
Bro.	John	Bro.	David
Lucius	Hanbury	Paulo	Bushe
—	—	No	1◇
1♡	1♠	4♡	No
No	Dble	End	

When East opened one diamond Brother Lucius decided to overcall on his strong four-card heart suit, keen to suggest this lead should West end in a spade contract. He soon found himself in four hearts doubled.

West, whose long hair was tied back with a rubber band, led a diamond and Brother Lucius ruffed in dummy. He paused to assess his prospects. If trumps were 3–2, the contract would be easy. He could draw two rounds of trumps, ruff the other diamond and establish the club suit. But what if trumps were 4–1? That line of play would be no good. He would lose control and go several down. It must be right to establish the side suit first.

Brother Lucius was about to play ace and another club when it occurred to him that on the bidding East might well hold all three clubs. How about the jack of clubs from dummy? Yes, that was a better idea.

East covered the jack with the king and declarer's ace was ruffed by West. Hanbury returned a spade but Brother Lucius had the hand well under control. He won the spade with dummy's ace, crossed to the ace of hearts for a second diamond ruff, played the king of trumps and established the club suit. The defenders could make just one club, one spade and two trump tricks – one down.

In the other room the auction took a different turn, the monastery East–West pair reaching the diamond game.

South	West	North	East
Julian	The	Mike	Bro.
Parker	Abbot	Trees	Xavier
—	—	No	1◇
2♣	Dble	5♣	Dble
No	5◇	No	No
Dble	End		

The Abbot entered the auction with a Sputnik double on the West cards. When his partner doubled five clubs, he was disinclined to pass in view of his unannounced five-card diamond support. His removal to five diamonds was doubled in turn by South.

Parker, the only student wearing a tie, led the ace of hearts, on which his partner petered with the 7, showing an even number of cards in the suit. Deciding there was little chance of beating the contract if declarer had a singleton heart, Parker continued with the king of hearts at trick 2. This set up two spade discards for declarer, saving him a guess in the suit. Eleven tricks were duly made.

"Switch to a trump and he has to take a view in spades, doesn't he?" complained the North player.

"Yes, but a trump switch relies on you having two spade tricks to beat the contract," replied Parker. "That didn't seem very likely."

"Why shouldn't I have something like king-jack-ten of spades?" persisted Trees, not happy with the way the match was going.

"If that's your holding, I'd have to switch to spades at trick two, wouldn't I?" replied Parker. "Otherwise declarer ditches two spades on the queen-jack of hearts, just losing two heart tricks."

Trees, still thinking that a trump switch was the obvious defence, reached for the next board. "Nice start to the weekend if we lose *this* match," he muttered.

The Abbot looked up sharply. Had his ears deceived him? Anyhow, the best way to deal with such insolence was to hand out a sound thrashing at the table. They would soon realise which of the two teams had had the easy draw.

This was the next board.

North–South game
Dealer South

```
                    ♠ K J 9 4
                    ♡ K 6
                    ◇ Q J 4
                    ♣ K J 8 2
   ♠ 10 8 5 3                        ♠ A
   ♡ 10 9 4 2          N             ♡ Q 7 5 3
   ◇ 9 6 3         W       E         ◇ 10 7 5 2
   ♣ 7 5               S             ♣ 10 9 4 3
                    ♠ Q 7 6 2
                    ♡ A J 8
                    ◇ A K 8
                    ♣ A Q 6
```

South	West	North	East
Julian	The	Mike	Bro.
Parker	Abbot	Trees	Xavier
2NT	No	3♣	No
3♠	No	6♠	End

Against six spades the Abbot led ♡ 10, won by declarer's jack. When a low spade was led from the South hand, the Abbot was quick to spot a text-book false card situation. With a smooth delivery that Lucius would have been proud of, he followed with ♠ 8. Dummy's king lost to the ace and East returned a heart to the dummy's king.

Parker, the students' captain, paused to consider his play in the trump suit. If West's 8 was a singleton, he should continue with the jack of trumps from dummy. Could the 8 possibly be a false card from ♠ 10 8 5 3? Surely a monk, a man of God, wouldn't contemplate such a deception.

Still uncertain, Parker crossed to hand with a diamond. When he led a second round of trumps towards dummy, the Abbot produced the 3.

He can't do this to me, thought Parker, turning to stare at the Abbot. Was the old codger really up to such an advanced false card or was he just making a fatuous trump peter from three small? The Abbot returned his stare in noncommittal fashion, waiting patiently for declarer's play from the dummy.

Parker finally made up his mind. "Play the jack," he said.

"One down," declared the Abbot, not waiting for Brother Xavier to follow to the trick. He leaned forward to inspect declarer's cards. "I'm surprised you didn't play that one in no-trumps," he observed. "That must be a better contract with so many points between you. In no-trumps if you misguess the spades you can fall back on the heart finesse."

The match was soon over. When the scores were compared, the monastery team found they had outscored the students by a handsome 37 IMPs.

"That impudent fellow in the striped shirt thought they'd come up with an easy draw," exclaimed the Abbot, filling in the result card with a flourish. "I must say I'm surprised he hadn't heard of us. That time we won the Benedictus Cup, they put the result in *The Daily Telegraph*, didn't they?"

"Yes, you cut it out and pinned it on the monastery notice board," replied Brother Lucius. "It's still there, I think. Gone a bit yellow over the years, of course."

The Abbot peered over his spectacles at Brother Lucius. "If we apply ourselves for the rest of this weekend, the notice board may well find itself freshly adorned," he declared. "Now, who's for a breath of sea air?"

It was wet and windy as the four monks hurried along the front at Eastbourne, searching for somewhere to eat.

"Ah, look over there!" said Brother Lucius. "The Golden Moon of Bengal. I haven't had a curry for ages."

"I'm not too keen on Indian food," declared the Abbot, the only one of the four to have an umbrella with him. "Shall we walk on and look for somewhere else? It's quite a pleasant evening."

He looked round to find the other three monks halfway across the road.

18

The Abbot's Brilliancy

The Abbot stared at the bill in disbelief. "£21.60p, just for four curries?" he exclaimed. "Good gracious, I used to get a curry for three or four shillings when I was a student."

"Well, it's a fair while since any of us have eaten in a restaurant," observed Brother Lucius. "I'm sure they've charged us correctly."

"Yes, Indians are supposed to be very good at mathematics," said Brother Xavier. "I read an article about it in the *Reader's Digest*."

The Abbot reached for his wallet. "Better leave a tip, I suppose," he grunted. "I'll round it up to 22 quid."

The four monks returned to the Grand Hotel to find that they had been drawn against a team of Yorkshire lifemasters in the next round of the Spring Foursomes.

"Could be worse," declared the Abbot. "Some of them are fair card players up there, but their bidding is hit-and-miss at the best of times."

The match was soon under way.

```
Love all                    ♠ A 5
Dealer North                ♡ 9 4
                            ◇ A K 10 6 5
                            ♣ 10 7 6 2
        ♠ Q 9 6 2                          ♠ 8 3
        ♡ Q 10 7 5 3          N            ♡ A J 6 2
        ◇ J 4            W         E        ◇ Q 9 8 3
        ♣ Q 5                S             ♣ J 9 4
                            ♠ K J 10 7 4
                            ♡ K 8
                            ◇ 7 2
                            ♣ A K 8 3
```

South	West	North	East
Bro.	Gerald	Bro.	Alan
Lucius	Manley	Paulo	Carfax
—	—	1◇	No
1♠	No	2♣	No
2♡	No	2♠	No
4♠	End		

With a promising trump holding, West decided to play a forcing game. His heart lead was won by East's ace and a heart was returned. Brother Lucius won with the king and paused to consider the play.

If he crossed to the ace of spades and took a losing trump finesse, West would force him in hearts and he would lose control unless the trumps were 3–3. If his trumps had been a little stronger – ♠ K J 10 9 x – he could have run the jack at this stage, leaving the ace in dummy to guard against a heart force.

Brother Lucius looked down at his hand, still undecided. It seemed to be one of those hands where he must play on the side suit first. What would happen if he played ace, king and another club? The defenders would win and play another heart, ruffed with dummy's low trump. Now the trumps would be blocked; that was no good.

Suddenly inspiration came to him. Of course! Why had it taken him so long to see it? He must play a low club from hand.

West played low on the club lead and East won with the jack. The heart return was ruffed with dummy's 5 and Brother Lucius cashed the ace of trumps. The lead was in dummy and these cards remained:

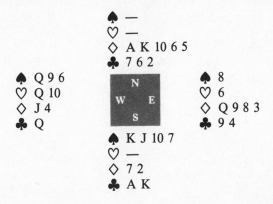

```
                    ♠ —
                    ♡ —
                    ♦ A K 10 6 5
                    ♣ 7 6 2
♠ Q 9 6                              ♠ 8
♡ Q 10          N                    ♡ 6
♦ J 4       W       E                ♦ Q 9 8 3
♣ Q             S                    ♣ 9 4
                    ♠ K J 10 7
                    ♡ —
                    ♦ 7 2
                    ♣ A K
```

Brother Lucius's next move was to cash the ace and king of diamonds to avoid being stranded in dummy later. Only then did he cross to hand in clubs to play the king and jack of trumps. West won and returned a heart but Brother Lucius was in control. He ruffed the heart, drew the last trump and claimed the contract.

The two Yorkshiremen eyed Brother Lucius curiously. How on earth had a monk managed to acquire such skill at card-play? Didn't they spend all their time pulling on bell-ropes and planting beetroot?

"Can't imagine why that took me so long," said Brother Lucius, smiling at his partner. "It was straightforward enough, really. I must have been half asleep."

Meanwhile in the other room, Brother Xavier and the Abbot were facing the Lever brothers.

"Long way for you to come, isn't it?" queried the Abbot. "Must be at least a five-hour drive down from Yorkshire. Anyhow, I thought you had your own heat up in the North."

"So we do," replied Ronald Lever, tapping the ash off his cigar. "The standard's tough up there, though. We thought we'd stand a better chance down here." He drew deeply on his cigar. "My go, is it? One no-trump."

This was the deal:

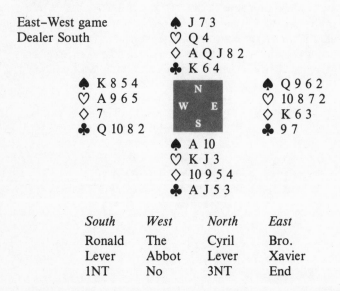

East–West game
Dealer South

```
              ♠ J 7 3
              ♡ Q 4
              ◇ A Q J 8 2
              ♣ K 6 4
♠ K 8 5 4                      ♠ Q 9 6 2
♡ A 9 6 5        N             ♡ 10 8 7 2
◇ 7          W       E         ◇ K 6 3
♣ Q 10 8 2       S             ♣ 9 7
              ♠ A 10
              ♡ K J 3
              ◇ 10 9 5 4
              ♣ A J 5 3
```

South	West	North	East
Ronald	The	Cyril	Bro.
Lever	Abbot	Lever	Xavier
1NT	No	3NT	End

The Abbot considered leading a spade but eventually turned to the slightly more solid club suit. Declarer won the club lead with the jack and ran ◇ 10 to East's king. Brother Xavier gazed at his hand. A club return was obviously too passive but which major should he play? Surely a spade. The best hope was that partner had a high card in each major and that the spade suit could be established.

When ♠ 2 appeared, Ronald Lever fingered his RAF moustache unhappily, suspecting that he had misplayed the hand. He tried the 10, but West won with the king and cleared the suit. Declarer went through the motions of running the diamond suit but it was a futile gesture. The defenders had no trouble with their discards and the contract went one down.

"Oh dear, what a shocker," apologised Ronald Lever. "It's a text-book hand; I should have played on hearts first, knocking out the stopper in the hand that can't attack the spades."

At the end of a lively but low-scoring first half the monastery team led by 12 IMPs. "No need for any heroics in the second half," announced the Abbot. "Just keep your heads down. Another 12 points will be more than adequate."

The second half was again full of action. This hand arrived late in the match:

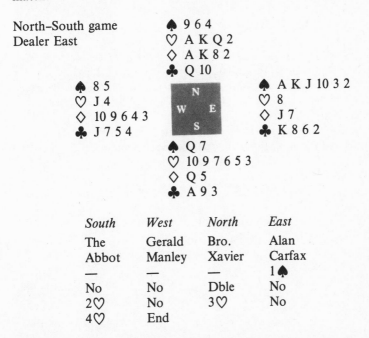

North–South game
Dealer East

```
              ♠ 9 6 4
              ♡ A K Q 2
              ◇ A K 8 2
              ♣ Q 10
♠ 8 5                        ♠ A K J 10 3 2
♡ J 4            N           ♡ 8
◇ 10 9 6 4 3   W   E         ◇ J 7
♣ J 7 5 4       S           ♣ K 8 6 2
              ♠ Q 7
              ♡ 10 9 7 6 5 3
              ◇ Q 5
              ♣ A 9 3
```

South	West	North	East
The	Gerald	Bro.	Alan
Abbot	Manley	Xavier	Carfax
—	—	—	1 ♠
No	No	Dble	No
2 ♡	No	3 ♡	No
4 ♡	End		

West led a spade against four hearts and East cashed two rounds before continuing with the jack. The Abbot ruffed with the 10 and was overruffed. West exited with a trump, which the Abbot won in dummy.

How could he avoid using a losing a club now? Surely the only chance was a minor-suit squeeze. Since the opening bid marked East with the king of clubs, the Abbot led the queen of clubs from dummy. East covered and the ace won the trick. The Abbot now ran the trump suit to produce this ending:

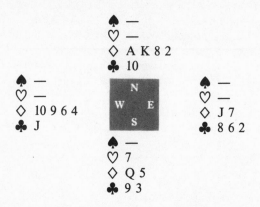

```
            ♠ —
            ♡ —
            ◇ A K 8 2
            ♣ 10
♠ —                        ♠ —
♡ —                        ♡ —
◇ 10 9 6 4                 ◇ J 7
♣ J                        ♣ 8 6 2
            ♠ —
            ♡ 7
            ◇ Q 5
            ♣ 9 3
```

The Abbot faced his hand with a flourish. "If either of you gentlemen holds four diamonds and the jack of clubs," he declared, "you will doubtless not be looking forward to the appearance of my last trump."

The player in the West seat returned his cards to the wallet, looking distinctly unimpressed by the style of the Abbot's claim.

"Director!" bellowed the Abbot.

An elderly director made his way from the far side of the room, squeezing through the mass of tables. "Yes?" he said, somewhat out of breath.

"Take the note of this hand, will you?" instructed the Abbot. "I'd like it entered for the brilliancy prize."

"Brilliancy prize?" queried the director. "Is there one? We haven't been told about it."

"I don't believe it," exclaimed the Abbot. "A hand like this comes up and there's no brilliancy prize? Check with the senior director, will you?"

The Abbot's Brilliancy

The Yorkshireman in the East seat was showing increasing signs of impatience. "If there is a brilliancy prize our declarer in the other room will probably win it by discarding a club loser on the third round of spades," he observed. "The contract was quite cold however the cards lay."

The Abbot stared blackly at his opponent. "I'm most obliged to you for pointing it out," he said. "Had you had the courtesy to mention it a little more promptly we could have avoided wasting this gentleman's time."

The match was soon over and the Abbot awaited the return of his other pair with every confidence. It was very rare for Lucius and Paulo to hand in a bad card.

"Ah, here they come," said the Abbot. "What news? Did you hold the fort?"

"One or two not so bad," replied Brother Lucius. "Paulo made a couple of thin games and they gave us an 800. How did you get on?"

The Abbot sat back in his chair with a satisfied smile. "Let's put it this way," he replied. "I don't think they'll bother driving so far in a year's time."

19

The Downfall of Brother Lucius

By Saturday night of the Spring Foursomes, a double elimination event, only four teams remained undefeated. Against all expectations, the St. Titus team was one of them.

"We're bound to meet a good team at this stage," declared the Abbot, striding anxiously towards the board displaying the draw. "It'll be the French team, I bet you."

The four monks looked at the top of the draw to see:

Undefeated Teams
Porter v Leclerc
Yorke-Smith v Mrs. Francis

"Might be worse, I suppose," said the Abbot, with a sideways glance.

"Francis?" queried Brother Paulo. "Are you knowing them, Abbot?"

"It wasn't the 'Francis' bit I was looking at," replied the Abbot. "It was the 'Mrs.'."

"We mustn't be too confident," warned Brother Lucius. "Aren't they the Sussex team that always does well in the er . . . what's it called? That women's event."

The match, played at opposite ends of the chandelier-lit Balmoral Suite, was soon in progress.

Game all
Dealer East

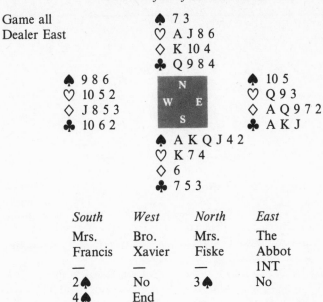

♠ 7 3
♡ A J 8 6
◊ K 10 4
♣ Q 9 8 4

♠ 9 8 6
♡ 10 5 2
◊ J 8 5 3
♣ 10 6 2

♠ 10 5
♡ Q 9 3
◊ A Q 9 7 2
♣ A K J

♠ A K Q J 4 2
♡ K 7 4
◊ 6
♣ 7 5 3

South	West	North	East
Mrs.	Bro.	Mrs.	The
Francis	Xavier	Fiske	Abbot
—	—	—	1NT
2♠	No	3♠	No
4♠	End		

The Abbot opened a strong no-trump but the two Sussex women still managed to climb to game. Brother Xavier led a trump against four spades and down went the dummy. Sarah Francis inspected its contents disapprovingly. What on earth was wrong with a call of 2NT on Audrey's cards? Game in no-trumps would be almost certain to succeed.

Mrs. Francis won the trump lead and drew a second round of trumps, noting the fall of East's 10. Temporarily abandoning the trump suit, she played a diamond to the 10.

The Abbot won with the queen and found himself in an awkward situation. He marked time by cashing the king of clubs, on which West played the 2. To play on hearts or clubs now would in effect give declarer two tricks. She would be able to draw the last trump, then take a discard on the thirteenth card of the suit led.

After considerable thought the Abbot played the ace of diamonds, ruffed by declarer. Mrs. Francis now ran the trump suit, arriving at this ending:

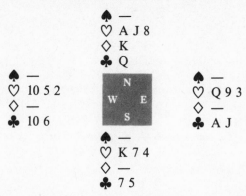

She then crossed to the ace of hearts and cashed the king of diamonds, forcing a club discard from East. It only remained to throw East in with the ace of clubs. The enforced heart return into the split tenace gave declarer her tenth trick.

"Nothing I could do about it," declared the Abbot, with a pained expression. "When I won that diamond trick it seems that I had three different ways of presenting declarer with the contract."

"Yes, poor lead, I'm afraid," said Brother Xavier. "I think a trump lead is the only one to let it through."

A few hands later Mrs. Francis arrived in another awkward game.

Love all
Dealer South

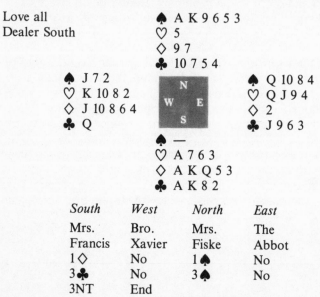

South	West	North	East
Mrs.	Bro.	Mrs.	The
Francis	Xavier	Fiske	Abbot
1◇	No	1♠	No
3♣	No	3♠	No
3NT	End		

For better or for worse, Mrs. Fiske decided against showing her club support. Against 3NT the monastery pair attacked in hearts, declarer winning the third round.

Even if diamonds broke 3–3 there would be only eight tricks available, since there was no entry to dummy. It therefore seemed that the club suit would be the key to the hand. If dummy could be reached on the fourth round of clubs, declarer would be able to enjoy the ace and king of spades.

Mrs. Francis cashed the ace of clubs and was not pleased to see the queen appear on her left. If that was a true card the dummy would be dead unless she could contrive some sort of endplay. The fall of the cards suggested that hearts were 4–4, so Mrs. Francis's next move was to exit in hearts. Brother Xavier won with the king and returned the jack of diamonds. When Mrs. Francis took the trick with the ace and cashed a second round of diamonds, these cards remained:

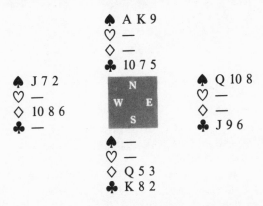

A club to the 7 and 9 left the Abbot with no satisfactory return. Eventually he played back a spade. Mrs. Francis cashed two tricks in the suit and then took the marked finesse in clubs. Nine tricks were there.

"Perhaps I should have raised your clubs," suggested Mrs. Fiske. "I suppose six clubs would have some play. On a 3–2 trump break, anyway."

Mrs. Francis, a retired schoolmistress, peered at her partner. "It may have escaped your notice, Audrey," she said, "but we ended up doing very nicely in no-trumps."

The Abbot stared curiously at Mrs. Francis. That had been pretty lively cardplay for a woman. Must have been a fluke, he decided.

At the interval the monastery team found they were adrift by 28 IMPs.

"Not exactly the half-time score I had in mind," reprimanded the Abbot. "Some of the fellows back home would find it no end of a joke if we lost to a team with four women in it."

The second half soon started. Lucius and Paulo had been playing a tight game, without actually gaining very much, when this hand arrived:

North–South game
Dealer North

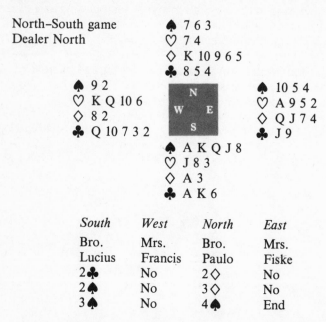

♠ 7 6 3
♡ 7 4
◇ K 10 9 6 5
♣ 8 5 4

♠ 9 2
♡ K Q 10 6
◇ 8 2
♣ Q 10 7 3 2

♠ 10 5 4
♡ A 9 5 2
◇ Q J 7 4
♣ J 9

♠ A K Q J 8
♡ J 8 3
◇ A 3
♣ A K 6

South	West	North	East
Bro.	Mrs.	Bro.	Mrs.
Lucius	Francis	Paulo	Fiske
2♣	No	2◇	No
2♠	No	3◇	No
3♠	No	4♠	End

The king of hearts was led against four spades and Mrs. Fiske, sitting East, paused briefly to consider her defence. She could overtake with the ace of hearts, but what then? A trump return? Declarer's bidding had indicated a very strong spade holding. It was surely too late to prevent him ruffing a heart. How about overtaking the heart and returning the jack of clubs? There seemed little point in that. Since dummy's diamonds posed no threat, declarer could never dispose of whatever club losers he had.

[138]

Eventually Mrs. Fiske came up with an imaginative idea. She would pretend she had a doubleton heart herself! Following this scheme, she overtook the king of hearts with the ace and fired back ♡ 2, which was covered by the jack and queen. Mrs. Francis was unsure of her partner's exact intentions but since it was obvious that a minor-suit switch could serve no purpose she continued with ♡ 10.

It was now Brother Lucius's turn to think. If hearts were 6–2, as seemed likely, he could not afford to ruff and be overruffed. There would then be an unavoidable club loser. He therefore discarded a club from dummy on the third round of hearts, intending to ruff a club later.

With three tricks in the bag, Mrs. Francis switched to a club. Brother Lucius won with the ace and drew two rounds of trumps before ruffing his club loser. Mrs. Fiske scored a well-deserved overruff and the contract went one down.

"Yes, well played, Audrey," said Mrs. Francis. "Sorry about the lead. If I start with a trump we can get it off without any trouble at all."

"I suppose I might have tried 3NT over three diamonds," observed Brother Lucius ruefully. "With hearts 4–4, it can't be touched."

The final comparison was soon in progress and not going too well for the monastery team.

"Minus 620," said the Abbot.

"Minus 100," said Brother Lucius.

"Another 13 IMPs down the drain!" exclaimed the Abbot. "What contract were you in?"

"Four spades," replied Brother Lucius innocently. "The same as in your room. No chance on a trump lead, is there?"

"Trump lead?" grunted the Abbot. "I led the king of hearts."

"Ah, the king of hearts," said Brother Lucius. "Well, that explains it."

20

The Abbot's Sense of Duty

"Have you heard the news?" whispered Brother Aelred as a group of monks entered the sunlit chapel for morning prayer. "The Abbot's team lost to those Sussex women in the Spring Fours!"

"That won't have put our superior in a very good mood," replied the bearded Brother Zac, chuckling to himself. "Looks like we'll have to keep our noses clean on his return. What was the winning margin?"

"No idea," said Brother Aelred, entering his usual pew and kneeling on the worn blue hassock. "He must have lost, though, or he would have 'phoned the result through. He did on all the other rounds."

Back in Eastbourne the Spring Foursomes was nearing its conclusion. The last two unbeaten teams were Leclerc, three of whose team had represented France in the Bermuda Bowl, and Mrs. Francis, who had beaten the St. Titus team in the previous round.

The Abbot's team now had to play another once-defeated side for a place in the semi-finals. Their opponents were four London rubber bridge players who were making a rare excursion into the world of duplicate.

This was an early board:

East–West game
Dealer South

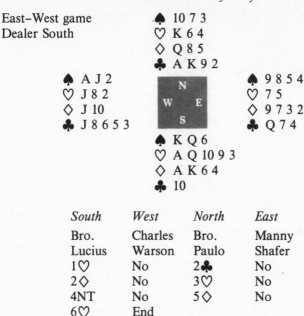

♠ 10 7 3
♡ K 6 4
◇ Q 8 5
♣ A K 9 2

♠ A J 2
♡ J 8 2
◇ J 10
♣ J 8 6 5 3

♠ 9 8 5 4
♡ 7 5
◇ 9 7 3 2
♣ Q 7 4

♠ K Q 6
♡ A Q 10 9 3
◇ A K 6 4
♣ 10

South	West	North	East
Bro.	Charles	Bro.	Manny
Lucius	Warson	Paulo	Shafer
1♡	No	2♣	No
2◇	No	3♡	No
4NT	No	5◇	No
6♡	End		

Charles Warson, well known in the aquarium world as a breeder of tinfoil barbs, led the jack of diamonds against six hearts. Brother Lucius won in hand, cashed the ace and king of trumps and led a spade to the king.

Warson was well aware of the theory that it was normally right to hold off the ace in these circumstances. However, when the moment came he could never steel himself to do it. At his club in London he played for high stakes and to let declarer make a slam by scoring the king from K x would be a capital offence. Warson won the king of spades with the ace and considered his return.

He had an easy exit in trumps, but might not that lead to a double squeeze? Yes. He would have to hold the jack of spades against dummy's 10; his partner might well have to keep a guard in diamonds. Neither defender would then be able to hold a club guard.

Hoping to prevent this possibility, Warson exited with a club, won by dummy's ace. Brother Lucius could not cash the king of clubs yet as there was no discard he could afford from hand. Instead, he ruffed a low club, isolating the club guard with West, and cashed all his trumps to arrive at this end position:

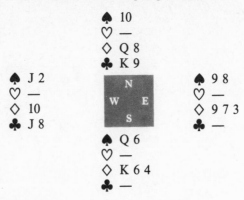

```
            ♠ 10
            ♡ —
            ◇ Q 8
            ♣ K 9

♠ J 2                        ♠ 9 8
♡ —          N               ♡ —
◇ 10      W     E            ◇ 9 7 3
♣ J 8         S              ♣ —

            ♠ Q 6
            ♡ —
            ◇ K 6 4
            ♣ —
```

When Brother Lucius cashed the king and queen of diamonds,
West had to discard a spade. The king of clubs then forced East to do
likewise and declarer scored two spade tricks to make his contract.

"How can you defend this way?" demanded Manny Shafer,
spreading his hands. "Hold off the ace of spades, he is finished."

Charles Warson returned his cards to the wallet. Tropical fish had
one admirable quality, he thought. Even if you forgot to feed them for
a week they would never abuse you or complain in any way.

"Yes, this must be a bad one for us," continued Shafer, running a
hand through his silvery hair. "Automatic to hold off the ace of
spades, partner. Absolutely automatic."

In a generally untidy match the points flowed freely in both
directions. The monastery team held a lead of just 3 IMPs when the
last set started.

The Abbot was put to the test on this board:

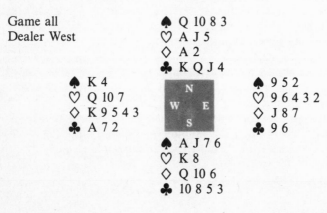

```
Game all            ♠ Q 10 8 3
Dealer West         ♡ A J 5
                    ◇ A 2
                    ♣ K Q J 4

♠ K 4                                ♠ 9 5 2
♡ Q 10 7           N                 ♡ 9 6 4 3 2
◇ K 9 5 4 3    W       E             ◇ J 8 7
♣ A 7 2              S               ♣ 9 6

                    ♠ A J 7 6
                    ♡ K 8
                    ◇ Q 10 6
                    ♣ 10 8 5 3
```

South	West	North	East
The	Ron	Bro.	Stan
Abbot	Gerner	Xavier	Feldmann
—	1◇	Dble	No
2♠	No	4♠	End

Ron Gerner, the London team's captain, expected most of the high cards to be to his left. He therefore decided to risk the deceptive lead of a low club. The Abbot won with dummy's king and East petered with the 9.

West's unorthodox lead had paid off in an unexpected way. It was obvious to the Abbot that a ruff in the club suit was imminent. What could be done about it? The Abbot stroked his chin thoughtfully, aware that the fate of the match might well be in his hands. Since the king of spades was obviously offside, he could play ace and another trump. Yes, that would save the ship if East had two black-suit doubletons.

Surveying dummy's assets once more, the Abbot spotted a further chance. He crossed to the king of hearts, finessed the jack of hearts successfully and discarded a diamond on the ace. Only then did he play ace and another trump.

West won with the king of trumps and gave his partner a club ruff. It brought the defenders little joy, since East was endplayed. When he returned a low diamond the Abbot lost no time in inserting the 10, forcing West's king. Ten tricks were now on view.

"Yes, I might have made that more difficult for you," said the West player, turning towards the Abbot. "If I play the queen on the second round of hearts, you might not like to risk a third round of the suit."

The Abbot smiled at this suggestion. "Such a gambit might be worth trying in a mixed pairs," he replied. "The sixth round of this competition is a somewhat different battleground, of course."

The final comparision was soon in progress.

"Plus 620," said the Abbot triumphantly. "One of my better efforts, I fancy."

"Minus 650," said Brother Lucius. "Diamond lead gave them the overtrick, I'm afraid."

"Overtrick?" exclaimed the Abbot. "On a club lead I had to stand on my head just to make it."

"Plus 150 on the next one anyway," said Brother Lucius. "They got to an absurd no-trump game."

"Yes, flat board," replied the Abbot. "Difficult to keep out of it. Now, what does that come to? Twelve in our direction, I make it, and three, four, nine, ten to them."

"Just enough!" exclaimed Brother Lucius. "We win by 5 IMPs."

"Who'd have believed we could reach the semi-finals?" said a delighted Brother Xavier. "This must call for a celebration, Abbot. Why don't we have another meal at that Indian restaurant near the pier?"

"An excellent idea," declared the Abbot, rising to his feet. "Duty first, though. I must put a call through to the monastery to check that everything's in order."

21

Incursus Gloriae Primus

The Abbot stared in disbelief at the board displaying the semifinal draw for the Spring Foursomes:–

Mrs. Francis v Yorke-Smith
Hagan v Leclerc

"Someone up there is certainly giving us a chance," he said.

"Someone up there is certainly giving Mrs. Francis a chance too," observed Brother Lucius. "They beat us quite easily a couple of rounds ago, don't forget."

"It'll be a different matter tonight," declared the Abbot. "They were hammered by the French this afternoon. 63 IMPs, I think it was."

"Really?" said Brother Xavier, chuckling to himself. "Well, they won't recover from a blasting like that in a hurry."

The two semi-finals were played in the red-carpeted Windsor room. An early board found Brother Paulo in 3NT.

Game all
Dealer East

```
              ♠ 10 7 2
              ♡ Q 3
              ◇ 9 6 3
              ♣ K Q J 8 7
♠ J 9 8 6 4 3              ♠ K 5
♡ 10 8          N          ♡ A K 9 6 2
◇ 7 5 4      W   E         ◇ 10 8 2
♣ 5 3           S          ♣ A 9 2
              ♠ A Q
              ♡ J 7 5 4
              ◇ A K Q J
              ♣ 10 6 4
```

South	West	North	East
Bro.	Gloria	Bro.	Joy
Paulo	Tunks	Lucius	Cahalan
—	—	—	1♡
1NT	No	3NT	End

West led ♡ 10 and Brother Paulo paused to assess his prospects. If he played low from dummy, East would let the 10 pass. The situation would then be hopeless unless the opening bid had been made on a four-carder.

"Play the queen," instructed Brother Paulo.

Mrs. Cahalan won with the king. If her heart holding had been a little stronger – ♡ A K 9 7 x – she might now have avoided a block by continuing with the ace or 9. As it was, she had little alternative but to continue with a low heart, the 6. Brother Paulo covered with the 7 and West's 8 won the trick. Mrs. Tunks now switched to spades, East's king forcing declarer's ace.

Brother Paulo turned to the club suit. When he played ♣ 10 and another club to the king, West petered to show her doubleton and East held up the ace. Brother Paulo was not yet dead. He cashed four rounds of diamonds and his remaining spade. When he exited with a third round of clubs, Mrs. Cahalan found that her last cards were the ace and 9 of hearts. Painful as it was, she had to surrender a ninth trick to Brother Paulo's jack of hearts.

"Yes, absolutely nothing we could do about it," said Mrs. Tunks. "It should be a flat board, Joy. I don't see why not."

At the other end of the room the Abbot and Brother Xavier were facing the stronger of the two ladies' pairs.

"You played the French team this afternoon, didn't you?" said the Abbot, taking his cards from the board. "How did you get on? Close game was it?"

"Very disappointing," replied Mrs. Francis. "Two unlucky boards in the first set and we never recovered. Lost by thirty-something in the end, I think. It's your call, Audrey."

Love all
Dealer North

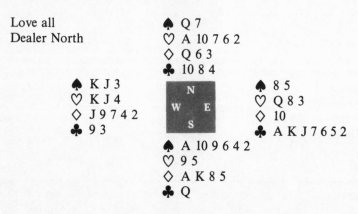

	♠ Q 7	
	♡ A 10 7 6 2	
	◇ Q 6 3	
	♣ 10 8 4	
♠ K J 3		♠ 8 5
♡ K J 4		♡ Q 8 3
◇ J 9 7 4 2		◇ 10
♣ 9 3		♣ A K J 7 6 5 2
	♠ A 10 9 6 4 2	
	♡ 9 5	
	◇ A K 8 5	
	♣ Q	

South	West	North	East
Sarah	Bro.	Audrey	The
Francis	Xavier	Fiske	Abbot
—	—	No	3♣
3♠	No	4♠	End

The ladies arrived in a thin spade game and Brother Xavier led ♣ 9 to the Abbot's king. Declarer ruffed the club continuation and led a low trump from hand, Brother Xavier going in with the king.

Unwilling to open one of the red suits, Brother Xavier decided to exit passively with a trump. Mrs. Francis was quick to take advantage of this lapse. She won the trick with dummy's queen and crossed to the ace of diamonds to draw the outstanding trump. She then ducked a round of hearts. Nothing could now prevent her from establishing dummy's heart suit and disposing of her losing diamond.

"I had the queen of hearts," exclaimed the Abbot with an anguished expression.

"Oh, dear," replied Brother Xavier. "Five clubs is very cheap in that case. Only one down if you guess the spades. You were a bit good for a three-bid weren't you?"

"What's that to do with it?" grunted the Abbot. "We should have beaten four spades. When you win with the king of trumps, you must switch to a heart."

"Yes, that beats it," agreed Mrs. Francis. "If I win with the ace there are insufficient entries to establish the heart suit. And if I duck, East will push through another club for a trump promotion."

"A heart switch was the only chance, wasn't it?" persisted the Abbot. "Declarer was marked with the ace of diamonds. If she had the queen of hearts as well, she was bound to be able to get the hearts moving."

"A diamond switch also beats it," said Mrs. Francis reflectively, "there's no way I can disentangle my entries."

Brother Xavier reached stoically for his score-card. What a pity the Abbot hadn't held his cards, he thought. If the Abbot was such a hot-shot at finding switches, why hadn't he switched to diamonds himself at trick two?

Despite this setback the monastery team found themselves 14 IMPs in the lead at half-time.

"What did I tell you?" said the Abbot. "We are 16 boards away from the most glorious moment in the monastery's history." He gazed happily at his team-mates. "Just imagine how proud St. Titus would be if he could see us here today."

Exchanges had been fairly even in the second half when the Abbot, sitting South, picked up this hand:

♠ A K
♡ 10 4
♢ A K 7
♣ A K Q 10 6 5

He opened with an Acol two clubs and Brother Xavier responded two spades. When he rebid three clubs, Brother Xavier raised him to four clubs. The Abbot studied his hand once more. It seemed fairly obvious to cue-bid four diamonds now, but this might give East the chance to double a four heart cue bid. If partner's hand was something like ♠ Q 10 9 7 6 2 ♡ A 8 ♢ J 3 ♣ 8 7 2, the fate of the grand might well depend on the opening lead. Unless trumps were 2–2, the ace of hearts would be the only entry to the blocked spades.

"Four no-trumps," said the Abbot, trying a different tack.

"Five clubs," replied Brother Xavier.

The Abbot stole a glance at his partner, somewhat amazed that he had found a positive response without the ace of hearts. "Six clubs," he said.

When this call ran round to the East player, she doubled. The implications of this manoeuvre did not escape the Abbot. Obviously East had a void in spades, dummy's first-bid suit.

"Six no-trumps," said the Abbot.

No further bidding ensued. This was the full hand:

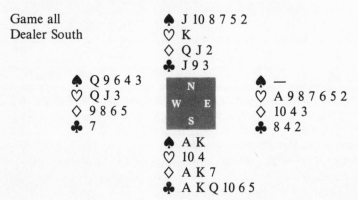

Game all
Dealer South

North:
♠ J 10 8 7 5 2
♡ K
♢ Q J 2
♣ J 9 3

West:
♠ Q 9 6 4 3
♡ Q J 3
♢ 9 8 6 5
♣ 7

East:
♠ —
♡ A 9 8 7 6 5 2
♢ 10 4 3
♣ 8 4 2

South:
♠ A K
♡ 10 4
♢ A K 7
♣ A K Q 10 6 5

South	West	North	East
The	Gloria	Bro.	Joy
Abbot	Tunks	Xavier	Cahalan
2♣	No	2♠	No
3♣	No	4♣	No
4NT	No	5♣	No
6♣	No	No	Dble
6NT	End		

West led ◇ 9 against 6NT and the Abbot, raising an eyebrow at the meagre dummy, won in hand. At least he had escaped a heart lead, he thought. What was Xavier thinking of, though, giving a positive on that load of rope? This board could cost them the match.

The Abbot cashed six rounds of clubs, discarding three spades from dummy. West discarded her remaining three diamonds and then had the unpleasant experience of seeing her partner throw ♡ 9. So, a heart lead would have beaten it, thought Mrs. Tunks. She would never hear the end of it if the slam succeeded.

The Abbot cashed the king of diamonds, arriving at this end position:

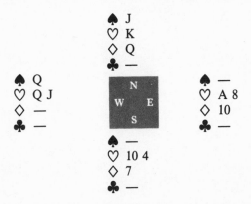

On the third round of diamonds West had to discard a heart honour. The Abbot, his pulse racing, now led the king of hearts from dummy. East won with the ace and had to concede the last trick to the Abbot's ♡ 10.

The Abbot mopped his forehead with a large white handkerchief. "An endplay worthy of the occasion," he announced.

"What a disastrous double, partner," exclaimed Mrs. Tunks, first into the attack. "I'd have led a spade anyhow against six clubs. It must go one down."

"Don't be absurd, Gloria," replied her partner. "With a void in dummy's suit *and* an ace in hand the double is absolutely obligatory."

"But how can it be right to drive them from a failing slam to a making one?" persisted Mrs. Tunks.

"Six no-trumps a making slam?" cried an exasperated Mrs. Cahalan. "Lead the obvious heart and they can't even make one no-trump!"

When scores were eventually compared, the monastery team found they had won the semi-final by 22 IMPs. In the final the next day they would meet the ante-post favourites, the French team captained by Henri Leclerc. It was hard to imagine a more exciting prospect.

"The gods will favour us tomorrow; I am sure of it," declared the Abbot, as his car sped through the empty streets of Eastbourne, heading for the Brotherhood of Bartholomew. "Trafalgar, Waterloo, Eastbourne. What a splendid hat-trick that would be!"

22

The Last Battlefield

The final of the Spring Foursomes had attracted an unusually large number of spectators. How would four brown-cassocked monks from the depths of Hampshire fare against the powerful French team, three of whose members had finished runners-up in the recent Bermuda Bowl?

It was difficult to get a view at the table where the Abbot and Brother Xavier were facing the crack French pair, Leclerc and Bougier. Battle commenced with this deal:

Game all
Dealer South

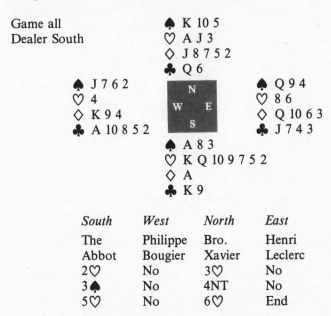

♠ K 10 5
♡ A J 3
◇ J 8 7 5 2
♣ Q 6

♠ J 7 6 2
♡ 4
◇ K 9 4
♣ A 10 8 5 2

♠ Q 9 4
♡ 8 6
◇ Q 10 6 3
♣ J 7 4 3

♠ A 8 3
♡ K Q 10 9 7 5 2
◇ A
♣ K 9

South	West	North	East
The	Philippe	Bro.	Henri
Abbot	Bougier	Xavier	Leclerc
2♡	No	3♡	No
3♠	No	4NT	No
5♡	No	6♡	End

The Abbot arrived in six hearts and West led the ace of clubs. East signalled with the 7 and West continued with another round of clubs, won by the Abbot's king.

The only real prospect of a twelfth trick was to establish a long diamond in dummy. The Abbot cashed the ace of diamonds and led ♡ 5 to dummy's jack. He then ruffed a diamond high and led ♡ 7 to dummy's ace. When he took a second diamond ruff, both defenders followed suit.

"They're all there now," said the Abbot, spreading his remaining cards on the table. "The 2 of hearts to dummy's 3 will allow me to ruff the last diamond good. Then I can cross to the king of spades to take a discard."

Leclerc caught his partner's eye. "Trump switch, he cannot do it," he said. "He is entry short."

"Yes, true," agreed his partner with a Gallic shrug. "But it was possible you had king of clubs."

Leclerc shook his head at this suggestion. "You think declarer would bid Blackwood with two losing clubs. It is not possible."

Bougier tried to recall the auction. "The Blackwood was from North, *n'est-ce pas?*" he said. "Anyhow the hand is on ice if declarer unblock king of clubs at trick one."

"*Oui, naturellement,*" muttered Leclerc, reaching for his score-card, "*mais . . .*"

The hand was soon replayed at the other table:

South	West	North	East
Jean-Luc	Bro.	Pierre	Bro.
Blocman	Lucius	Limoux	Paulo
1♣	No	2◇	No
2♡	No	3♣	No
3♡	No	3♠	No
6♡	End		

The young French pair also reached six hearts, on a Precision sequence. South's two hearts was an asking bid and the response denied four controls but promised at least three hearts to a top honour. When Blocman heard a spade cue-bid, he blasted into the slam.

With no attractive lead, Brother Lucius decided to advance his singleton trump. Declarer won with the 10 and unblocked the ace of diamonds. He then led a low club towards the queen.

Brother Lucius paused to consider his defence. Declarer was marked with the ace of spades and the king of clubs. If his shape was 3-6-1-3, nothing could be done. Declarer would be able to ruff his club loser and establish a diamond for a spade discard. Strangely, there was a chance for the defence if declarer had a slightly better distribution, 3-7-1-2. Yes, the game must be to go in with the ace of clubs. That would kill one of the entries to dummy if declarer held K x in the suit.

Blocman's dark eyes flashed when the ace of clubs appeared. What could one do against such hot defence? He won the club return with the king and used dummy's two trump entries to ruff two diamonds, isolating the diamond guard. It brought him no joy. Brother Lucius retained three spades and the slam went one down.

"It was good slam," Blocman informed his partner. "Trump is the only lead to hurt me."

No more fireworks occurred in the first set, which ended with the monastery team 9 IMPs in the lead. There was an expectant buzz from the onlookers as the players resumed their seats. The Abbot, who had lost most of his own hair at an early age, gazed curiously at the young Frenchman in the West seat. How absurd to have hair pouring out of your forehead like that, he thought.

"Same system as your other pair?" queried the Abbot in an intimidating tone.

"No, we play strong club," replied Limoux. "Five-card majors *en principe*; one diamond may be short suit."

The Abbot reached for their convention card. "Ah, Precision," he said. "Why didn't you say so? We have heard of it, you know. Our monastery is not completely isolated from the world."

He looked up at the kibitzers to see if this sportive thrust had been well received. Meeting only a few stony glances, he leaned forward to extract his cards from the wallet.

North–South game
Dealer East

	♠ Q 10 7 2	
	♡ 6 5	
	◇ A Q 6	
	♣ Q 8 7 3	

♠ 9 6 4		♠ 5
♡ 8 3	N W E S	♡ K J 9 7 4 2
◇ J 10 7 5 2		◇ K 8 4
♣ A 10 5		♣ K 9 2

	♠ A K J 8 3	
	♡ A Q 10	
	◇ 9 3	
	♣ J 6 4	

South	*West*	*North*	*East*
The	Pierre	Bro.	Jean-Luc
Abbot	Limoux	Xavier	Blocman
—	—	—	2♡
2♠	No	4♠	End

[153]

Limoux led ♡ 8 against four spades and the Abbot won with the 10. What were the prospects? The club honours were probably divided since West would doubtless have led one if he held both. It was possible, though, that the king of diamonds was offside. The three missing kings and the jack of hearts would make up a 10-count and East's weak two had shown 6–10. What could be done in that case? Ah yes, of course . . . an elimination.

The Abbot drew three rounds of trumps, then finessed the ♡ Q and cashed the ace, discarding a diamond from dummy. The ace and queen of diamonds followed, throwing East on lead with the king.

The Abbot faced his cards. "Choose your poison," he said. "You must open the club suit or give a ruff-and-discard."

The Frenchman nodded and returned his cards to the wallet. "Your other pair play weak two?" he enquired. "I think it is more difficult for you if heart position is not made so obvious."

"No, we all play Acol twos," replied the Abbot happily. "They might find a one bid on your cards but I doubt it."

The West player displayed his cards to the other three players. "After one-spade – three spade – four spade I might still lead heart doubleton," he said, "or could be jack of diamonds."

Meanwhile the other French pair had an awkward bidding problem.

Love all
Dealer North

	♠ 9 4 2	
	♡ A 10 8 2	
	◊ A K Q 9	
	♣ Q 3	
♠ A Q J 8 6 5		♠ 10
♡ K Q 9 3		♡ J 6 5 4
◊ 8		◊ J 10 6 3 2
♣ 10 5		♣ 8 4 2
	♠ K 7 3	
	♡ 7	
	◊ 7 5 4	
	♣ A K J 9 7 6	

South	West	North	East
Henri	Bro.	Philippe	Bro.
Leclerc	Lucius	Bougier	Paulo
—	—	1NT	No
3♣	3♠	No	No
4♣	No	4◊	No
4♡	No	5♣	End

Leclerc might well have bid 3NT at his second turn, leaving any further move to his partner. As it was, he took a rosy view of his hand and the French pair bypassed the simple 3NT, arriving in five clubs. West led the king of hearts; Leclerc won in dummy and ruffed a heart. He then crossed to the queen of clubs and ruffed another heart with the 9. Brother Lucius unblocked the queen on this trick, anxious to avoid a subsequent endplay.

The French declarer drew a second round of trumps with the ace, crossed to the ace of diamonds and ruffed dummy's last heart. These cards remained:

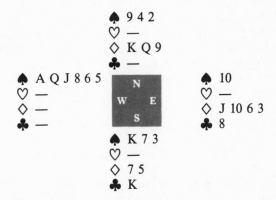

```
                  ♠ 9 4 2
                  ♡ —
                  ◇ K Q 9
                  ♣ —
   ♠ A Q J 8 6 5       N       ♠ 10
   ♡ —                         ♡ —
   ◇ —            W       E    ◇ J 10 6 3
   ♣ —                S       ♣ 8
                  ♠ K 7 3
                  ♡ —
                  ◇ 7 5
                  ♣ K
```

Leclerc could count West for four hearts, two or three clubs and probably six spades. It was clear that the diamond suit was not breaking. On the king of clubs Leclerc discarded a diamond from dummy, keeping the spade holding intact. When two rounds of diamonds followed, Brother Lucius was unwilling to reduce himself to ♠ A Q J. If he did, an endplay would surely follow. In desperation he threw the jack of spades, retaining ♠ A Q 8.

It was to no avail. Leclerc led a low spade from dummy, covering East's 10 with the king. A few seconds later dummy's ♠ 9 claimed the eleventh trick.

"You played it well," said Brother Lucius, congratulating his opponent. "I think we must hope that our other pair find an alternative spot somewhere, partner."

"Three no-trumps, you mean?" said Leclerc, laughing. "Yes, that would have been a better spot, indeed."

The half-time comparison was soon in progress.

"Plus 660," said the Abbot.

"Ah, that's a relief," said Brother Lucius. "You were in no-trumps. They played in five clubs. Minus 600."

"Could you have beaten it, then?" asked the Abbot, wondering what had prompted Lucius's concern.

"No," replied Brother Lucius. "It was quite a tricky hand to play, that's all."

"No need to worry on that account," said the Abbot stiffly. "Now this may be a good one. Plus 620."

"Yes, flat," said Brother Lucius.

"You led a heart?"

"Afraid so," replied Brother Lucius. "He couldn't really go wrong after that."

The Abbot totted up the score. "Still 6 IMPs ahead," he reported. "I trust the selectors will bear this performance in mind when the next Bermuda Bowl comes round."

An early hand in the third set tested Leclerc, the French captain.

Game all
Dealer West

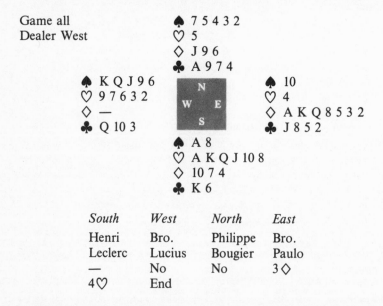

	♠ 7 5 4 3 2	
	♡ 5	
	◇ J 9 6	
	♣ A 9 7 4	
♠ K Q J 9 6		♠ 10
♡ 9 7 6 3 2		♡ 4
◇ —		◇ A K Q 8 5 3 2
♣ Q 10 3		♣ J 8 5 2
	♠ A 8	
	♡ A K Q J 10 8	
	◇ 10 7 4	
	♣ K 6	

South	West	North	East
Henri	Bro.	Philippe	Bro.
Leclerc	Lucius	Bougier	Paulo
—	No	No	3 ◇
4 ♡	End		

Brother Lucius led the king of spades against four hearts and Leclerc won in hand. Prospects were poor. If West held five spades and five clubs, it might be possible to squeeze him. But only if East co-operated by cashing his other two diamond winners when he was thrown in. It seemed more likely that East would switch to clubs, breaking the squeeze.

In any event the first step must be to draw trumps. Leclerc cashed the ace of hearts, followed by the king. Bougier played dummy's trump on the first round, then reached for a spade.

"Diamond, diamond!" reprimanded Leclerc, just in time.

Declarer drew trumps in three more rounds, discarding two more diamonds and a club from the table. He then played the king and ace of clubs and ruffed a club. Finally he exited with ♠ 8. Brother Lucius cashed three tricks in this suit, declarer discarding diamonds, then at the last trick had to lead his ♠ 6 to dummy's 7. Ten tricks were there.

"A good one for third and fifth leads," observed Brother Lucius with a rueful smile. "If I do decide to lead a spade, only the 6 is good enough."

At the other table the Abbot was in the driving seat, trying to steer home a difficult 3NT contract.

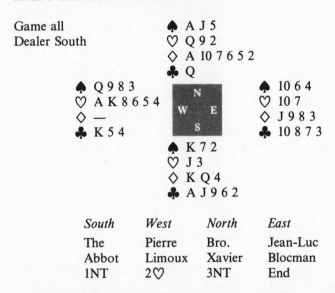

Game all
Dealer South

	♠ A J 5	
	♡ Q 9 2	
	◇ A 10 7 6 5 2	
	♣ Q	
♠ Q 9 8 3		♠ 10 6 4
♡ A K 8 6 5 4		♡ 10 7
◇ —		◇ J 9 8 3
♣ K 5 4		♣ 10 8 7 3
	♠ K 7 2	
	♡ J 3	
	◇ K Q 4	
	♣ A J 9 6 2	

South	*West*	*North*	*East*
The	Pierre	Bro.	Jean-Luc
Abbot	Limoux	Xavier	Blocman
1NT	2♡	3NT	End

Uncertain what rewards a double of two hearts would bring, Brother Xavier opted for 3NT. This bid, directly over West's intervention, promised a heart stop in his system.

Limoux, playing attitude leads, led ♡ 4 to the 2, 7 and jack. When the Abbot cashed the king of diamonds West showed out, discarding a club. The hand had changed complexion in an instant and the Abbot sat back in his chair to consider the matter. What could be done now?

Deciding that he might manage an endplay if West held the missing black honours, the Abbot continued with the queen and ace of diamonds. Limoux parted with a heart and then another club, baring his king.

When the Abbot crossed to the king of spades, finessed the jack and cashed the ace, West followed suit with the 3, 9 and queen. These cards were still at large:

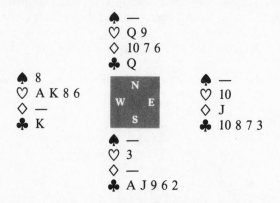

The Abbot was now at the crossroads. Which defender had hidden the missing spade? If West had it, his king of clubs must now be bare. If East had it, West could be endplayed with the queen of hearts to give declarer two club tricks.

The Abbot could see no clue to guide him. Even so, since the decision was a crucial one, he sat motionless in his seat for a further two minutes, hoping for inspiration. "Queen of hearts," he said at last.

West won and cashed three more hearts, the Abbot discarding dummy's queen of clubs to clear the way to his own ace–jack.

With no change of expression Limoux placed ♠ 8 on the table. "The last one is yours," he said.

The Abbot stared at the spade, overwhelmed with disappointment. "You bared the king of clubs?" he said.

"The king of clubs always single, I think you say," replied the Frenchman, reaching for his cigarettes.

These two deals cost the monastery team dearly and the French started the last set 9 IMPs in the lead. Exchanges had been even when this hand occurred near the end of the match.

North–South game
Dealer North

	♠ Q 10 4
	♡ A 10 8 6 5
	◇ A 7
	♣ 7 6 3

♠ K 7 2	N	♠ 9 8 6 5
♡ J 7 4 3	W E	♡ Q 9 2
◇ 9 4	S	◇ K Q 5 2
♣ K 8 5 2		♣ J 9

	♠ A J 3
	♡ K
	◇ J 10 8 6 3
	♣ A Q 10 4

South	West	North	East
Jean-Luc	Bro.	Pierre	Bro.
Blocman	Paulo	Limoux	Lucius
—	—	No	No
1◇	No	1♡	No
1NT	No	2NT	No
3NT	End		

Against 3NT Brother Paulo led ♣ 2 to the jack and queen. When Blocman played ace and another diamond, Brother Lucius followed in unconcerned fashion with the 2 and 5.

Blocman knew the expert play at this point. If diamonds were 3–3, any card from hand would do. If West held a doubleton honour, it was vital to keep his J 10 intact. With a glance at the kibitzers he played ◇ 8 from hand. Brother Paulo won with the 9.

East's jack of clubs at trick one had denied the 10, marking declarer with ♣ A Q 10. Brother Paulo therefore switched to hearts. After this sparkling start by the defence, declarer was doomed. He managed to establish a long diamond eventually, but he could not prevent the defenders scoring three diamond tricks and the black kings to put him one down.

Blocman turned a respectful eye towards Brother Lucius. "You ducked from K Q x x?" he said. "The right play, of course."

"Not too difficult," replied Brother Lucius. "Partner might hold J x, for one thing."

"True," said Blocman. He smiled to himself. "Also it has been known for declarer to put in the 9 from J 9 x x x."

It was clear that the match was desperately close. The French players, in their corner, were the first to arrive at a score. They broke into an agitated babble of conversation.

At the other end of the room the monastery team were checking their arithmetic feverishly. "I don't believe it," exclaimed the Abbot. "We win by 2 IMPs, I make it."

"Yes, 24–13 in this set," agreed an excited Brother Xavier, "and we were 9 behind. We've done the impossible!"

The French captain, Henri Leclerc, approached the table and bowed to the Abbot. "You played very well. All of you," he said.

The Abbot rose to his feet, beaming triumphantly. "Well, we expected a hard fight," he said, "and you certainly didn't disappoint us. It was anybody's game."

"Quite so," agreed Leclerc. "As unbeaten team, of course, we have the right to eight extra boards. Shall we start straight away?"

"Eh?" said the Abbot.

23

The Abbot's Final Shot

"I'm absolutely exhausted, Abbot," whispered Brother Xavier, as they awaited the arrival of their opponents. "I don't think I can last another eight boards."

"How do you think the rest of us feel?" grunted the Abbot. "Just keep going for one more hour. We can still win this one."

The French pair, looking fresh as daisies, soon arrived. Play restarted with this deal:

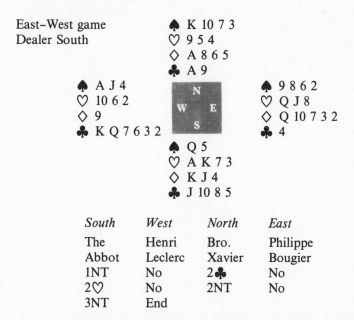

East–West game
Dealer South

	♠ K 10 7 3	
	♡ 9 5 4	
	◇ A 8 6 5	
	♣ A 9	
♠ A J 4		♠ 9 8 6 2
♡ 10 6 2		♡ Q J 8
◇ 9		◇ Q 10 7 3 2
♣ K Q 7 6 3 2		♣ 4
	♠ Q 5	
	♡ A K 7 3	
	◇ K J 4	
	♣ J 10 8 5	

South	West	North	East
The	Henri	Bro.	Philippe
Abbot	Leclerc	Xavier	Bougier
1NT	No	2♣	No
2♡	No	2NT	No
3NT	End		

Playing attitude leads, Leclerc led ♣ 2 against 3NT. Dummy's 9 won the first trick and the Abbot played a spade to the queen, Leclerc ducking smoothly.

The Abbot, his eyelids becoming heavier by the minute, tried to summon his concentration. There seemed to be no hurry to test the diamond suit. The best move at this stage was surely to duck a heart, establishing some prospects in that suit.

When the Abbot led a low heart towards the dummy's 9, West pounced with his 10. A low club to dummy's ace left Leclerc with four winners in the suit. The Abbot could now count seven tricks – eight tricks if the hearts divided. Since the diamond finesse was into the dangerous hand, it seemed obvious to try his luck in the spade suit first.

He crossed to the ace of hearts and led a spade, intending to finesse the 10. The opportunity for such a manoeuvre never presented itself. To the Abbot's horror, West produced the ace of spades and proceeded to cash four club winners.

Somewhat dazed, the Abbot sat back in his chair. "Where was the queen of diamonds?" he enquired.

"Over there, I think," replied Leclerc, pointing across the table with an apologetic air.

Brother Xavier leaned over to view the East hand. "Oh dear," he said. "Hearts were 3–3 as well, Abbot."

"I can't help that," said the Abbot gruffly. "Playing on spades was far and away the best chance the way the play had gone."

In the other room Brother Lucius and Brother Paulo were facing the younger of the French pairs.

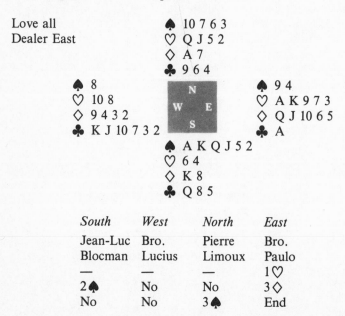

Love all
Dealer East

	♠ 10 7 6 3	
	♡ Q J 5 2	
	◇ A 7	
	♣ 9 6 4	
♠ 8		♠ 9 4
♡ 10 8	N	♡ A K 9 7 3
◇ 9 4 3 2	W E	◇ Q J 10 6 5
♣ K J 10 7 3 2	S	♣ A
	♠ A K Q J 5 2	
	♡ 6 4	
	◇ K 8	
	♣ Q 8 5	

South	West	North	East
Jean-Luc	Bro.	Pierre	Bro.
Blocman	Lucius	Limoux	Paulo
—	—	—	1♡
2♠	No	No	3◇
No	No	3♠	End

The French pair were playing intermediate jump overcalls and Limoux displayed good judgement in passing two spades originally. Many 7-point hands would be worth a call, but it was unlikely here that his heart honours would pull much weight.

The ♡ 10 was led, covered by the queen and king. Brother Paulo then cashed the ace of clubs, West signalling with the jack. Cashing the ace of hearts would be a poor play now, it seemed to Brother Paulo. There was very little chance of a trump promotion; the play would merely establish dummy's jack of hearts for a discard. Even if West had started with a singleton heart, there would be no way for declarer to dispose of his two heart losers. Brother Paulo therefore switched to a trump at trick 3.

Blocman was pleasantly surprised to have escaped a club continuation. Presumably East had no further club to return. He drew trumps in two rounds, eliminated the diamond suit and then led ♡ 6 from hand, calling for dummy's 2.

The defenders could do nothing. If West's ♡ 8 took the trick, he would have to give a ruff-and-discard or surrender a trick in clubs. If instead East won the heart trick, he would have to give a ruff-and-discard or concede a trick to dummy's jack of hearts. Brother Paulo eventually let his partner's 8 win the trick. West's subsequent play of the club king gave Blocman a ninth trick.

"Sorry, Paulo," said Brother Lucius. "Looks like four diamonds is a make. I should have given you a raise."

Blocman reached mechanically for his packet of Gitanes. The first 32 boards had been something of a nightmare. At last it seemed that the law of the jungle was beginning to assert itself.

It was shortly after three in the morning when the Abbot extracted his cards for the last hand. Prospects of winning the match were grim. He and Xavier had clocked up two obviously bad boards and there was only one plus score on their card. Although Lucius and Paulo had often rescued them from such a poor card in the past, it was too much to expect this against the present opposition.

Deciding that he would have to create a swing himself on the last board, the Abbot inspected his hand. It was a depressingly flat 8-count:

♠ Q 9 2   ♡ K 8 4   ◇ J 8 6 5   ♣ Q 10 3

His heart sank. How could anyone work a miracle with that load of horse manure? The first two players passed and the Abbot steeled himself for action.

"One spade," he said. If the great Plum Meredith could open three-card spade suits, why shouldn't he?

The Frenchman in the West seat overcalled 1NT and Brother Xavier, sitting North, studied his hand thoughtfully.

The Abbot was not too worried. He had opened in the third seat at favourable vulnerability and the Frenchman had made a strong call. Surely even Xavier would exercise some discretion in the circumstances.

"Four spades," said Brother Xavier.

Damn fool, thought the Abbot.

"Double," said Bougier.

There was no further bidding and West led the king of trumps. This was the full deal:

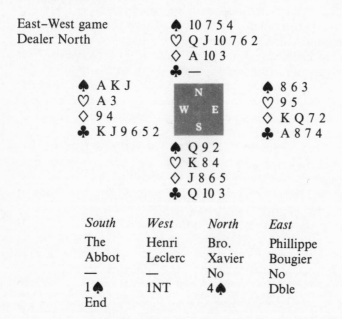

East–West game
Dealer North

♠ 10 7 5 4
♡ Q J 10 7 6 2
◇ A 10 3
♣ —

♠ A K J
♡ A 3
◇ 9 4
♣ K J 9 6 5 2

♠ 8 6 3
♡ 9 5
◇ K Q 7 2
♣ A 8 7 4

♠ Q 9 2
♡ K 8 4
◇ J 8 6 5
♣ Q 10 3

South	West	North	East
The	Henri	Bro.	Phillippe
Abbot	Leclerc	Xavier	Bougier
—	—	No	No
1♠	1NT	4♠	Dble
End			

After winning the first trick with the king of spades, Leclerc switched to ◇ 9. When the Abbot played low from dummy, East won with the queen and returned a trump to the 9 and jack. Leclerc cashed the ace of spades, leaving just one trump in dummy, and switched to a club, which ran to East's ace. When the defenders continued mercilessly with their club suit, the Abbot held off dummy's last trump until the fourth round, hoping that the defender with the heart ace would have no clubs remaining.

[164]

It was not to be. When the Abbot played on hearts, Leclerc won with the ace and cashed two more club tricks. The Abbot eventually scored a spade, a heart and a diamond, going down 1300.

"Yes, six clubs is there without a heart lead," he observed. "We may gain 2 IMPs on the board but I doubt if it will be enough."

The French pair departed and were soon replaced by the other monastery pair.

Brother Lucius shook his head as he sat down. "No good, I'm afraid," he reported. "They made all the games they were in and we got too high on the spade hand."

The Abbot, although downcast at the defeat, was relieved to find that his own bad boards had not been solely responsible. He glanced at Lucius's scorecard and gave a sad shake of the head. "I don't think our results are sparkling enough to make up for a card like that," he declared. "It rather looks as if this is the end of the road."

The French team had won the match by a comfortable 36 IMPs. Their captain, Henri Leclerc, approached the Abbot and gave him a compassionate embrace.

"What bad fortune," he said. "You are playing so well for so long and then. . ."

The Abbot, who could think of nothing to say, suffered the stranglehold in silence. Eventually the Frenchman released his grasp.

"As you have made such brave fight, I have suggestion to make," said Leclerc. "If we are taking the cup back to Paris, it will be difficult for us returning it after one year."

The Abbot pricked up his ears.

"Perhaps you would be so kind to look after the trophy for us," continued Leclerc. "You are deserving it, really. You beat us over the 32 boards."

A gleam came to the Abbot's eye. The Spring Foursomes Cup on the sideboard of his study for a whole year? What a prospect!

"It'll be a tight squeeze in my little car," he said. "But we'll fit it in somehow."

24

The Abbot's Unusual Pose

The Abbot, holding the Spring Foursomes trophy victoriously aloft, bared his teeth in a triumphant smile. "Get a move on!" he said, maintaining his smile with the technique of an expert ventriloquist. "This cup weighs a ton."

"Don't move, Abbot; I'm nearly ready," replied Brother Michael, adjusting the tripod of the ancient monastery camera. "Ah, hang on a moment. I can't remember if I put a flash-bulb in."

Eventually the Abbot's arms gave way. With a muttered imprecation he bent down to deposit the cup on the floor. A blinding flash illuminated the room.

"It worked!" exclaimed Brother Michael, emerging from behind the camera. "I hope I got you all right, Abbot. The photo's for that article you're sending to the *Hampshire Chronicle*, isn't it?"

"That was my intention," replied the Abbot heavily. "Whether their readers would be interested in a close-up of the top of my head is another matter entirely. I'll have to find someone more competent to have a go after tonight's pairs."

The Abbot stormed out of the refectory and made his way to the main card-room, where the Tuesday night pairs was about to start.

The first round placed the Abbot and Brother Lucius against the leading pair from the novitiate. Such encounters were always keenly fought since tales of a success against the Abbot were worth several rounds of free drinks in the novitiate buttery.

Love all
Dealer North

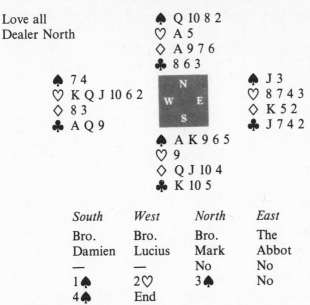

♠ Q 10 8 2
♡ A 5
♢ A 9 7 6
♣ 8 6 3

♠ 7 4
♡ K Q J 10 6 2
♢ 8 3
♣ A Q 9

♠ J 3
♡ 8 7 4 3
♢ K 5 2
♣ J 7 4 2

♠ A K 9 6 5
♡ 9
♢ Q J 10 4
♣ K 10 5

South	West	North	East
Bro.	Bro.	Bro.	The
Damien	Lucius	Mark	Abbot
—	—	No	No
1♠	2♡	3♠	No
4♠	End		

Against four spades Brother Lucius led the king of hearts, won in dummy. Brother Damien ruffed a heart in hand, drew trumps in two rounds and ran the queen of diamonds. The Abbot won with the king and made the obvious switch of a low club to the ten and queen. Brother Lucius had a safe exit in diamonds, so declarer eventually lost two more club tricks to go one down.

"Oh dear, oh dear," declared the Abbot with a sad shake of the head. "It's like playing in a different world after last weekend."

"Did I misplay it, then, Abbot?" enquired Brother Damien.

"He still hasn't seen it!" exclaimed the Abbot. "Ace and another diamond; that's the way to play it. Then Lucius has no safe exit when he wins the first club."

"Yes, that's right, isn't it, Damien?" said the young North player. "If the king of diamonds is onside, you can afford to give up a diamond trick. Your clubs give you a guaranteed elimination position."

"I'd have played it that way at teams, of course," replied Brother Damien. "But at pairs I'm sure of eleven tricks if the king of diamonds is right. What would you have done, Lucius?"

"Well, it's a close one," replied Brother Lucius. "But at pairs I think. . ."

"Let's get on," interrupted the Abbot. "If we give these youngsters a bridge lesson every hand, Lucius, we'll still be here at midnight. Pass over the next board, will you?"

North–South game
Dealer East.

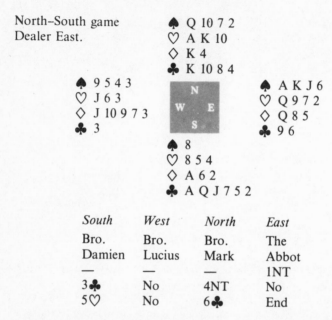

```
                    ♠ Q 10 7 2
                    ♡ A K 10
                    ◇ K 4
                    ♣ K 10 8 4
♠ 9 5 4 3                          ♠ A K J 6
♡ J 6 3                            ♡ Q 9 7 2
◇ J 10 9 7 3                       ◇ Q 8 5
♣ 3                               ♣ 9 6
                    ♠ 8
                    ♡ 8 5 4
                    ◇ A 6 2
                    ♣ A Q J 7 5 2
```

South	West	North	East
Bro.	Bro.	Bro.	The
Damien	Lucius	Mark	Abbot
—	—	—	1NT
3♣	No	4NT	No
5♡	No	6♣	End

When the Abbot opened 1NT Brother Damien could not bring himself to pass on the South hand. Since two clubs would have been Aspro, he chanced his arm with three clubs. Reckoning that he had four or five tricks to contribute to a club contract, Brother Mark advanced to the six level.

Brother Lucius led the jack of diamonds, declarer winning in hand. After drawing two rounds of trumps, Brother Damien tried the effect of a low spade from dummy. The Abbot, who could scarcely risk playing low, went in with the jack, which held the trick. Brother Lucius petered with the 5, showing an even number of spades.

The Abbot could not play another high spade now or he would be exposed to a subsequent ruffing finesse. A heart seemed equally risky since declarer might well hold the jack. Giving the matter no further thought, the Abbot exited with a diamond to the dummy's bare king.

Brother Damien now led the queen of spades, which was covered and ruffed. After ruffing his last diamond on the table, declarer ran the trump suit. This ending resulted:

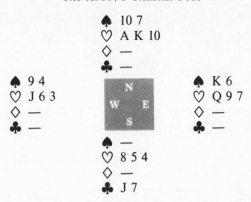

♠ 10 7
♡ A K 10
◇ —
♣ —

♠ 9 4
♡ J 6 3
◇ —
♣ —

♠ K 6
♡ Q 9 7
◇ —
♣ —

♠ —
♡ 8 5 4
◇ —
♣ J 7

On the penultimate trump West could not afford a spade or his 9 would be exposed to a pin by dummy's 10. He therefore discarded a heart. The ♡ 10 was thrown from dummy and the Abbot, unwilling to bare the king of spades, also let go a heart.

Brother Damien now unblocked the ace and king of hearts, returned to hand with a spade ruff and cashed the established heart. Twelve tricks were in the bag.

"What happened there?" exclaimed a delighted Brother Mark. "Great play, partner!"

"Yes, we can stop that one," observed Brother Lucius. "It wasn't easy for you, Abbot, but. . ."

"I know, I know," said the Abbot. "Play low on the first round of spades. How can I tell where the 9 is?"

"No, I didn't mean that," said Brother Lucius. "When you're in with the jack of spades, you must switch to a heart. He needed two heart entries for that ending."

"Return a heart?" exclaimed the Abbot. "You must be joking. If declarer had the jack, I'd be led away by the men in white coats."

"If declarer had the jack of hearts, he would have eliminated diamonds before throwing you in," replied Brother Lucius. "Then you'd have been forced to play a heart."

"A superficial analysis," declared the Abbot. "The chance of a member of the novitiate stumbling into a squeeze ending like that must be at least 25–1 against. 50–1, probably. Forgetting to eliminate a side suit, on the other hand, is almost odds-on at their level."

The Abbot paused for breath. "Ah, the other tables are still in play," he observed, levering himself out of his chair. "If you've no more fatuous comments to make on the last hand, Lucius, you can do something useful for me in the refectory. Come on!"

25

Brother Mark's Heavy Load

"Have you seen the Abbot's article in the *Hampshire Chronicle*?" asked Brother Xavier, crossing the quadrangle on his way to the card-room.

"So far I've been spared that pleasure," replied Brother Lucius. "Usual sort of thing, is it? Implied that the Spring Foursomes was an individual event?"

"More or less," said Brother Xavier. "There's a large picture of him holding the cup in the air and no mention of the other players in the team, nor of the fact that the French team actually beat us in the final."

"Par for the course," said Brother Lucius, smiling at his colleague. "It'll cause some amusement in the novitiate, I dare say. Make a treasured cutting for their prayer books."

"Yes, and I'll tell you another thing," continued Brother Xavier. "The novices have all found out about that hand where the Abbot psyched a spade opening on queen-to-three and went for 1300. Queen-to-three jokes are all the rage there, apparently."

"So I heard from Paulo yesterday," replied Brother Lucius. "If anyone opens one spade in the novitiate duplicate, his partner knocks on the table and warns the opponents that it may be on queen-to-three."

"Really?" said Brother Xavier, much amused. "If our superior got wind of that there'd be some fireworks."

The two monks climbed the west-wing staircase and stepped into the main card-room, where the Abbot and Brother Paulo were already seated at the £1 table.

"At last!" exclaimed the Abbot. "What kept you so long?"

"We were paying our devotions in the chapel," replied Brother Lucius. "Praying for the mission in the Congo Basin, actually. Lost track of the time."

"Such lack of consideration for others is hardly a good example to our younger brethren," grunted the Abbot. "Very thoughtless."

He spread the pack and the other three players selected a card. Brother Xavier drew the highest card and, in accordance with monastery custom, took the seat opposite the Abbot. This was the first hand.

Brother Mark's Heavy Load

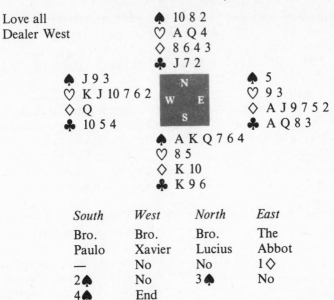

Love all
Dealer West

```
          ♠ 10 8 2
          ♡ A Q 4
          ◇ 8 6 4 3
          ♣ J 7 2
♠ J 9 3                    ♠ 5
♡ K J 10 7 6 2      N      ♡ 9 3
◇ Q              W     E    ◇ A J 9 7 5 2
♣ 10 5 4            S       ♣ A Q 8 3
          ♠ A K Q 7 6 4
          ♡ 8 5
          ◇ K 10
          ♣ K 9 6
```

South	West	North	East
Bro.	Bro.	Bro.	The
Paulo	Xavier	Lucius	Abbot
—	No	No	1◇
2♠	No	3♠	No
4♠	End		

Brother Xavier led the queen of diamonds against four spades and the Abbot won with the ace. When ◇ 2 was returned, Brother Xavier ruffed declarer's king and continued with a low club to the Abbot's ace.

The Abbot sat back in his chair, well satisfied with the defence so far. What now? Surely there was a chance of a trump promotion. The Abbot returned the jack of diamonds, but Brother Paulo ruffed high and drew the outstanding trumps in two rounds. Two further rounds of trumps led to this end position:

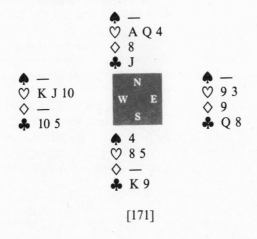

```
          ♠ —
          ♡ A Q 4
          ◇ 8
          ♣ J
♠ —                        ♠ —
♡ K J 10           N       ♡ 9 3
◇ —             W     E     ◇ 9
♣ 10 5             S       ♣ Q 8
          ♠ 4
          ♡ 8 5
          ◇ —
          ♣ K 9
```

On the last trump West, with one eye on dummy's ♡ A Q 4, decided to let a club go. Dummy and East both discarded a heart. Brother Paulo then finessed the queen of hearts and cashed the ace, squeezing the Abbot in the minor suits. When the Abbot threw a club, Brother Paulo overtook the jack of clubs with the king, scoring two tricks in the suit and making the game exactly.

"I was hoping you had better trumps, there," said the Abbot, looking severely across the table. "I can't think why you returned a club with such bad trumps. Surely it's obvious that a heart switch gives nothing away?"

"That's true, Abbot," replied Brother Xavier. "But you gave me the *two* of diamonds. I'm afraid I took it as a McKenney signal for clubs."

"Of course it was," barked the Abbot. "That doesn't mean you shouldn't use your common sense with only J x of trumps left."

Brother Paulo turned towards the Abbot. "I think perhaps you can still beat it on club return," he said. "If you play queen of clubs instead of the ace, there is no squeeze for me. My last trump would force Xavier to bare the 10 of clubs, but I can't clear a second club trick. You would have at least one diamond winner."

"I'm not interested in double-dummy recoveries from partner's errors," replied the Abbot sternly. "How would it help Brother Xavier to improve his game if I kept on compensating for his mistakes on this side of the table? Anyhow, 3NT was absolutely frigid. Why you were fooling around in spades, I can't imagine."

The very next hand found Brother Paulo in game once more.

North–South game
Dealer North

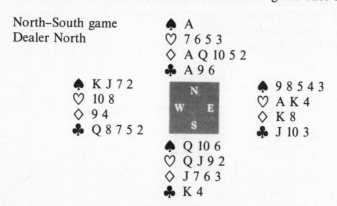

```
North-South game        ♠ A
Dealer North            ♡ 7 6 5 3
                        ◇ A Q 10 5 2
                        ♣ A 9 6
    ♠ K J 7 2                         ♠ 9 8 5 4 3
    ♡ 10 8            N                ♡ A K 4
    ◇ 9 4          W     E             ◇ K 8
    ♣ Q 8 7 5 2       S              ♣ J 10 3
                        ♠ Q 10 6
                        ♡ Q J 9 2
                        ◇ J 7 6 3
                        ♣ K 4
```

South	West	North	East
Bro.	Bro.	Bro.	The
Paulo	Xavier	Lucius	Abbot
—	—	1◇	No
1♡	No	3♡	No
4♡	End		

The Abbot decided not to overcall on his poor spade suit, and the opponents reached game in an uncontested auction. Expecting a good diamond suit in dummy, Brother Xavier made the attacking lead of ♠2, won by dummy's ace. When a low trump was led from the table the Abbot rose with the king. He returned another spade to the 10 and jack, ruffed in the dummy.

Brother Paulo paused to calculate his next move. If he played a second round of trumps at this stage, the defenders might win and play a third round. They would then be in a position to cash a spade winner if the king of diamonds was offside.

What if he crossed to the king of clubs, ruffed his last spade and then played a second round of trumps? That was no better. The defenders would force him with a fourth round of spades when they took the ace of trumps. He would have to draw the defenders' last trump and East would be able to cash the thirteenth spade, if the diamond finesse proved to be wrong.

"Come on, come on. This isn't the Gold Cup," muttered the Abbot. "You're in the dummy."

It seemed to Brother Paulo that he would have to risk playing on diamonds before he tackled the trump suit again. Yes, that must be the answer. He crossed to the king of clubs and finessed the queen of diamonds. The Abbot won the trick with the king but found that the contract was now impregnable. If he played two more rounds of trumps, declarer would simply ditch his spade loser on the long diamond. The Abbot tried a spade return instead, but Brother Paulo ruffed in dummy and led a trump, remaining well in control.

A few seconds later the Italian was totting up the score. "That's the sort of rubber I am liking," he observed gleefully. "Nine, do you make it?"

The Abbot reached for his wallet. "I don't know what I've done to deserve a couple of hands like that," he declared, as he counted out the notes. "If I called it highway robbery I wouldn't be far from the mark."

"Yes, there wasn't much you could do on the last one," said Brother Paulo. Holding up the king of diamonds would have been worth a try, he thought. But such a play would never occur to the Abbot.

"Did that photograph I took of you turn out all right, Abbot?" said Brother Lucius, with an innocent expression.

"What?" replied the Abbot, spreading the pack for the next cut. "Oh yes, I believe they did use it in this week's *Chronicle*. I thought I owed it to the team to send in a small piece on our efforts in the Spring Foursomes."

"Ah, that is explaining it, then," said Brother Paulo. "I saw Brother Mark carrying a heavy load of newspapers into your study this morning."

"Yes, I ordered a few extra copies," replied the Abbot. "Perhaps one of you could help me distribute them after Matins tomorrow?"

26

Boys Will Be Boys

As the Abbot walked down the path from the monastery chapel the soaring beauty of Bach's Toccata in G sharp faded away behind him.

"Amazing," he said. "How can anyone play the organ like that and yet be so completely clueless at the bridge table?"

"One of the world's great mysteries, I agree," said Brother Xavier. "Mind you, it's rather unfair the way people malign Brother Aelred's mental processes. It's not his fault he's got such a small head, is it?"

"I suppose not," replied the Abbot. "Still, there was a hand he played last week that really defied belief. He was in three spades doubled and. . ."

"Yes, I heard about it from Lucius," said Brother Xavier. "By the way, this league match we're playing tonight, who is it against?"

"Masefield School, just outside Romsey," replied the Abbot, as they walked past the buttery into the cloisters. "They were promoted from the second division last season apparently. Should be a 20–0 touch but you never can tell."

That evening the monastery team were welcomed at the gates of Masefield public school by the junior geography master, Alan Cutforth. "The boys have really been looking forward to this encounter," he informed the Abbot. "They seem quite confident, actually. I've been giving them extra practice sessions all week."

"Have you indeed?" replied the Abbot. "Did you hear that, Lucius? We ought to arrange something like that ourselves."

Two tables had been set up in the gymnasium and the match was soon under way.

North–South game
Dealer South

South	West	North	East
Bro.	*Piers-*	*Bro.*	*Kumar*
Lucius	Devenish	Paulo	Pattani
2NT	No	6NT	End

Brother Lucius ended in 6NT and Steven Piers-Devenish, an athletic six-footer who was captain of the school rugby team, led ♣ 10.

Brother Lucius surveyed the dummy. It seemed a routine enough contract. The slam was in danger only if East held all four diamonds. He won the club lead in dummy and led a diamond to the 7 and king. When West discarded a spade on this trick it was time to reconsider the hand. The chance of a spade–diamond squeeze was surely too remote. The best prospect seemed to be an endplay on East.

Brother Lucius cashed four rounds of clubs and the young Indian in the East seat discarded two spades. Everyone followed to the king of spades, leaving this end position:

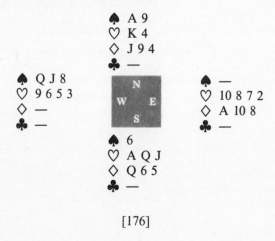

When the ace of spades was cashed, East was forced to part with a heart. Brother Lucius now cashed three rounds of hearts and led a diamond to the jack. East won with the ace but then had to lead from the 10, giving declarer a twelfth trick.

"Oh, what a clever play, indeed!" exclaimed Kumar Pattani. "I doubt our lads will be making that one. What you think, Devvers?"

"They certainly won't make it if they get to six diamonds," replied Piers-Devenish. "The way those two idiots normally bid, I expect they'll be two off in seven diamonds!"

"Oh dear, in that case it will be two off doubled," observed Pattani learnedly. "With A 10 8 x of trumps East would double, most clearly."

Brother Lucius gazed curiously at the two opponents. Did they really represent the cream of Britain's present-day youth?

At the other end of the gymnasium, next to the vaulting horse, the younger of the two Curzon brothers was playing in four spades.

Love all
Dealer East

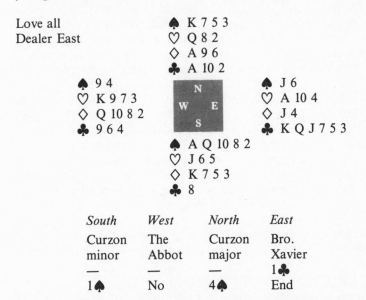

	♠ K 7 5 3	
	♡ Q 8 2	
	◇ A 9 6	
	♣ A 10 2	
♠ 9 4		♠ J 6
♡ K 9 7 3		♡ A 10 4
◇ Q 10 8 2		◇ J 4
♣ 9 6 4		♣ K Q J 7 5 3
	♠ A Q 10 8 2	
	♡ J 6 5	
	◇ K 7 5 3	
	♣ 8	

South	West	North	East
Curzon minor	The Abbot	Curzon major	Bro. Xavier
—	—	—	1♣
1♠	No	4♠	End

Against four spades the Abbot led ♣ 9, won in dummy with the ace. Curzon minor, a fourth-former known universally as 'Brainbox', inspected dummy's assets. If diamonds were 3–3 he could eventually discard a heart from dummy and take a heart ruff for his tenth trick. What if the diamonds were 4–2, though? He had plenty of trumps. Perhaps an elimination would be possible.

[177]

At trick 2 declarer ruffed a club in hand. He then drew trumps in two rounds and ruffed another club. Next came the king of diamonds and a diamond to the 9. Brother Xavier won with the jack and found that he had no good return. A ruff-and-discard would obviously give declarer a trick, so he had to try a low heart. Curzon minor displayed his remaining cards with a youthful flourish and claimed the contract.

"Yes, a straightforward enough elimination," declared the Abbot. "We had a similar hand in our match against the French world championship team a few weeks ago."

"Can't we beat this one, though, Abbot?" said Brother Xavier. "If you go in with the queen on the second round of diamonds, I don't get endplayed with the jack."

"That's right," said Curzon minor, turning towards the Abbot. "A Crocodile Coup. You could have worked it out. I would finesse against the queen if I had the K J of diamonds, so your partner was marked with the jack."

"Curzon minor!" snapped the geography master, who had been watching the play. "It's extremely bad form to criticise an opponent's play. *Manners makyth man*, remember. I'm so sorry, Abbot. I do apologise."

"We have similar problems with some of the younger members of the novitiate," replied the Abbot, reaching for his scorecard. "Maintaining a courteous attitude at the table is every bit as important as the play itself, of course." He shook his head sadly. "All one can do is try to teach by example, but it's an unrewarding task."

Curzon major caught his brother's attention. "I'm not sure your analysis was right, anyhow," he said. "Surely declarer *would* cash the king of diamonds first if he held K J x x. Then he can cross to the ace and lead back towards the jack, gaining when West holds Q x."

"Quite so," said the Abbot, sorting his cards for the next deal. "I hesitated to point that out myself, but this young man is right."

At half-time the monastery team were 11 IMPs in the lead.

"Just eleven?" queried the Abbot, checking his arithmetic. "That's not much use against a pack of schoolboys. We need to win by 56 IMPs to get the full 20 victory points."

Brother Lucius exchanged a glance with his partner, Brother Paulo. They'd had several good boards themselves and had expected a substantial lead. "Yes, I'm sorry, Abbot," he said. "That two spade contract on board 12 was where we dropped the points at our table. If I find the trump lead from Q x we can hold it to eight tricks."

Pretending not to hear this remark, the Abbot indicated with his forefinger that Lucius and Paulo should depart for the next set.

[178]

Alan Cutforth spent the next fifteen minutes marking the Lower Third's maps of the Nile Delta. With a sigh he put the last exercise book on the neat pile beside him and looked up to see how the match was progressing. This hand had just been dealt.

Game all
Dealer South

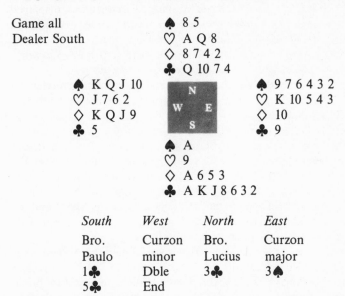

```
                    ♠ 8 5
                    ♡ A Q 8
                    ♢ 8 7 4 2
                    ♣ Q 10 7 4
  ♠ K Q J 10          N          ♠ 9 7 6 4 3 2
  ♡ J 7 6 2      W        E      ♡ K 10 5 4 3
  ♢ K Q J 9                      ♢ 10
  ♣ 5                  S         ♣ 9
                    ♠ A
                    ♡ 9
                    ♢ A 6 5 3
                    ♣ A K J 8 6 3 2
```

South	West	North	East
Bro.	Curzon	Bro.	Curzon
Paulo	minor	Lucius	major
1♣	Dble	3♣	3♠
5♣	End		

Curzon minor led the king of spades against five clubs. Brother Paulo won with the ace and crossed to the queen of trumps to ruff dummy's remaining spade. He then exited innocently with ♢ 3. His contract was at risk only if the diamonds were 4–1. In that case there was a fair chance that East would win the trick with a bare diamond honour. He would then have to lead into dummy's heart tenace or give a ruff-and-discard.

Curzon minor inspected ♢ 3 for a few seconds, then went in with the king. When the 10 appeared from his partner he turned triumphantly towards Alan Cutforth. "Did you see that, Sir?" he exclaimed. "A Crocodile Coup! There was a similar position on one hand in the first half. The oppo didn't spot it, fortunately."

Feeling well pleased with himself, Curzon minor continued with the queen of diamonds. This was the card Brother Paulo had been hoping to see. He took the trick with the ace and ran ♡ 9. East won with the 10 but had no sound return. Brother Paulo faced his hand, claiming the remainder.

"Which of you is having the heart king?" he enquired.

"Over there," replied Curzon minor, wondering what had prompted the question. "It makes no difference, does it? We can't avoid the endplay."

"Well, it is quite hard for me if you are playing small heart when you win the king of diamonds," replied the Italian. "Why should I play the 8? I don't know yet if diamonds are 4–1."

"Quite so," agreed Alan Cutforth, leaning forward. "That was very out of place, Curzon minor, commending your own defensive play in the middle of a hand. *Pride cometh before a fall*, remember."

Curzon minor was unabashed. "I bet you wouldn't have found that king of diamonds play, Sir," he said. "I wonder if they'll beat it at the other table."

Brother Lucius glanced over to the far side of the gymnasium where the heads of the other players could just be viewed over the vaulting horse. "I see that the Abbot is sitting West," he observed. "I can't believe he'll miss two Crocodile Coups in a row."

When the third set was scored it transpired that the Abbot had not been put to the test.

"Plus 600," said Brother Paulo hopefully.

"Yes, we found the sacrifice in five spades," said the Abbot. "Just 500 away. Three IMPs to us."

"Ah, well done, Abbot," said Brother Lucius, tongue in cheek.

"Well, I doubled and Xavier was 6–5 in the majors," replied the Abbot. "Fairly obvious to press on with that sort of shape. Not to these young lads, I dare say."

The monastery team's lead had increased to 16 IMPs but this was still well short of the Abbot's expectations. He gave a final exhortation to his troops and battle resumed.

Love all
Dealer North

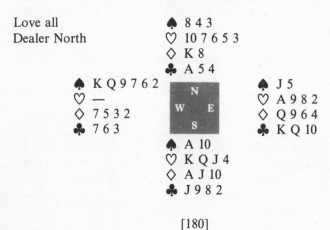

```
                    ♠ 8 4 3
                    ♡ 10 7 6 5 3
                    ◇ K 8
                    ♣ A 5 4
  ♠ K Q 9 7 6 2                   ♠ J 5
  ♡ —               N             ♡ A 9 8 2
  ◇ 7 5 3 2       W   E           ◇ Q 9 6 4
  ♣ 7 6 3           S             ♣ K Q 10
                    ♠ A 10
                    ♡ K Q J 4
                    ◇ A J 10
                    ♣ J 9 8 2
```

South	West	North	East
Piers-	Bro.	Kumar	The
Devenish	Xavier	Pattani	Abbot
—	—	No	1NT
Dble	2♡	Dble	No
No	2♠	No	No
3♡	No	4♡	End

When the Abbot was doubled in 1NT Brother Xavier attempted to obscure the issue with a bid of two hearts. The school pair proved well capable of dealing with this. After exposing the psyche with a penalty double, they bid competently to the game in hearts. Brother Xavier led the king of spades and declarer won with the ace.

West's lead was presumably from the king–queen, thought Piers-Devenish, so East's 1NT marked him with all the other honour cards. When the king of hearts was led, the Abbot held up the ace. Declarer's next move was to cross to the king of diamonds, finesse the jack of diamonds and cash the ace, discarding a club. Nine tricks were on view and it seemed that a spade ruff in hand would provide a tenth. With this in mind, Piers-Devenish exited with ♠ 10 to West's queen.

The club return was won by dummy's ace, leaving this end position:

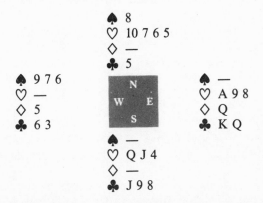

```
                    ♠ 8
                    ♡ 10 7 6 5
                    ◇ —
                    ♣ 5
  ♠ 9 7 6                          ♠ —
  ♡ —            N                 ♡ A 9 8
  ◇ 5        W       E             ◇ Q
  ♣ 6 3          S                 ♣ K Q
                    ♠ —
                    ♡ Q J 4
                    ◇ —
                    ♣ J 9 8
```

When ♠ 8 was led, the Abbot discarded the queen of clubs and declarer ruffed in hand with the 4. The Abbot won the queen of trumps return, cashed the king of clubs and exited to declarer's bare jack of trumps. There was no way to reach dummy without promoting the Abbot's last trump, so the contract went one down.

"Not a discard that would occur to many, that queen of clubs," declared the Abbot. "Only way to beat it, of course. I doubt if they'll find it in the other room."

Lucius and Paulo wouldn't give them the chance thought Brother Xavier. There had been no need to play on diamonds so early. If declarer had simply given up a spade at trick 2, or after the king of hearts, nothing could have defeated him.

The next few hands went fairly well for the school pair. They seemed to be in with a chance of closing the gap when the final board of the match was placed on the table.

North–South game
Dealer North

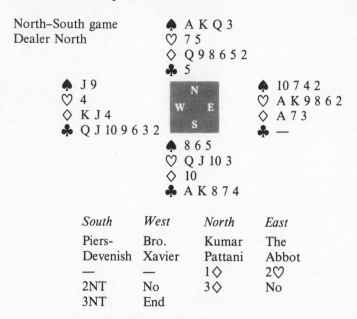

♠ A K Q 3
♡ 7 5
◇ Q 9 8 6 5 2
♣ 5

♠ J 9
♡ 4
◇ K J 4
♣ Q J 10 9 6 3 2

♠ 10 7 4 2
♡ A K 9 8 6 2
◇ A 7 3
♣ —

♠ 8 6 5
♡ Q J 10 3
◇ 10
♣ A K 8 7 4

South	West	North	East
Piers-	Bro.	Kumar	The
Devenish	Xavier	Pattani	Abbot
—	—	1◇	2♡
2NT	No	3◇	No
3NT	End		

Alan Cutforth winced at the 3NT call. What an atrocity! Had Piers-Devenish paid *any* attention to his careful instruction of the past three weeks?

Against 3NT Brother Xavier led the queen of clubs, won by declarer's king. When ◇ 10 was run to the Abbot's hand he decided, for no very good reason, to duck. Declarer now crossed to the spade ace and led the queen of diamonds. Again without giving the matter much thought, the Abbot went up with the ace and returned a low heart, won by declarer's queen.

It was now a simple matter for Piers-Devenish to cross to the king of spades and establish the diamond suit. As West had only clubs to return when he won the king of diamonds, declarer's final tally was an amazing ten tricks.

"I couldn't leave you in diamonds," explained Piers-Devenish. "I only had a singleton."

Brother Xavier looked towards the Abbot with an anguished expression. "We can still beat it, even after you duck the ace of diamonds," he said. "Let me win the second round of diamonds with the king. Then you can discard the ace of diamonds on my club continuation and. . ."

The Abbot wasn't listening; he was already halfway across the gymnasium. "Not one of Xavier's better matches," he muttered, as he arrived at his team-mates' table. "Don't ask him about the last hand, whatever you do. I don't want to embarrass him."

The monastery team had won the match by just 1 IMP, a 10–10 draw in victory points. Alan Cutforth was in a buoyant mood as he accompanied the monastery team towards the Abbot's car. "An excellent tussle, Abbot, I'm sure you agree," he said, pushing open the school gates to let the monastery team through. "I didn't think you'd give our boys such a close fight. That last 3NT hand was a remarkable one, Abbot. I think if you take the ace of diamonds immediately you can . . ."

"Yes, thank you so much, Mr. Cutthorpe," said the Abbot, attempting to close the gate on the geography master's fingers. "And please thank Matron for the refreshments. Paste sandwiches have always been a weakness of mine."

The team soon reached the Abbot's car. "Oh dear, Abbot," exclaimed Brother Xavier. "It seems that some prankster from the school has let all your tyres down. Look at that!"

"Just what we needed on such a freezing cold night," grunted the Abbot. "You'll find a foot-pump in the boot, Xavier. The rest of us will get in the car. No point in the whole team catching pneumonia, is there?"